CHILDREN'S MENTAL HEALTH & EMOTIONAL WELL-BEING IN PRIMARY SCHOOL

Sara Miller McCune founded SAGE Publishing in 1965 to support the dissemination of usable knowledge and educate a global community. SAGE publishes more than 1000 journals and over 800 new books each year, spanning a wide range of subject areas. Our growing selection of library products includes archives, data, case studies and video. SAGE remains majority owned by our founder and after her lifetime will become owned by a charitable trust that secures the company's continued independence.

Los Angeles | London | New Delhi | Singapore | Washington DC | Melbourne

CHILDREN'S MENTAL HEALTH & EMOTIONAL WELL-BEING IN PRIMARY SCHOOLS

COLIN HOWARD, MADDIE BURTON, DENISSE LEVERMORE & RACHEL BARRELL

Learning Matters
An imprint of SAGE Publications Ltd
1 Oliver's Yard
55 City Road
London EC1Y 1SP

SAGE Publications Inc.
2455 Teller Road
Thousand Oaks, California 91320

SAGE Publications India Pvt Ltd
B 1/I 1 Mohan Cooperative Industrial Area
Mathura Road
New Delhi 110 044

SAGE Publications Asia-Pacific Pte Ltd
3 Church Street
#10-04 Samsung Hub
Singapore 049483

Editor: Amy Thornton
Production controller: Chris Marke
Project management: Swales and Willis Ltd, Exeter,
Devon
Marketing manager: Dilhara Attygalle
Cover design: Wendy Scott
Typeset by: C&M Digitals (P) Ltd, Chennai, India
Printed by: CPI Group (UK) Ltd, Croydon, CR0 4YY

Library of Congress Control Number: 2017936982

British Library Cataloguing in Publication Data

A catalogue record for this book is available from the
British Library

ISBN 978-1-4739-7578-1
ISBN 978-1-4739-7579-8 (pbk)

At SAGE we take sustainability seriously. Most of our products are printed in the UK using FSC papers and boards.
When we print overseas we ensure sustainable papers are used as measured by the PREPS grading system.
We undertake an annual audit to monitor our sustainability.

CONTENTS

About the authors   vi

Acknowledgements   vii

1   Mental health and emotional well-being   1

2   Promoting a whole school approach   24

3   Children and young people's behaviour: what is being
    communicated and how should we respond?   43

4   Self-esteem   62

5   Bullying, social media and promoting resilience   83

6   The influence of family mental health   102

7   The need for inclusion   117

8   Who's looking after whom?   132

Index   147

ABOUT THE AUTHORS

Colin Howard is a Senior Primary Lecturer in Initial Teacher Education at the University of Worcester. He has been involved in primary education for over 24 years, of which 14 years have been spent as a successful head teacher in both small village and large primary school settings. He has a strong research interest which includes primary science, aspects of professional practice and teachers' professional identity. He is a SIAMS inspector of the Diocese of Hereford.

Maddie Burton is a Registered Mental Health Nurse and for several years worked in both inpatient and community CAMHS. She has an MA in Psychodynamic Approaches to Working with Adolescents from The Tavistock and University of East London. She is currently Senior Lecturer in Child and Adolescent Mental Health at the University of Worcester. She continues to maintain close links with CAMHS practice and works with schools from a CAMH perspective. She holds membership of the Association for Child and Adolescent Mental Health and the Association for Infant Mental Health. Maddie's research interests include suicide and self-harm in children and young people, and infant, maternal and parental mental health. Maddie is also a Fellow of the Higher Education Academy.

Denisse Levermore is a Senior Lecturer in Child and Adolescent Mental Health at the University of Worcester. Her qualifications include: Registered General Nurse, Registered Children's Nurse, Diploma in Social Work and MSc Child and Adolescent Mental Health. Denisse has over 15 years' experience of working with vulnerable families and child and adolescent mental health in her previous roles as a Nurse Therapist within CAMHS and as a Family Nurse within Family Nurse Partnership. She maintains her clinical practice within CAMHS currently by way of an honorary contract, undertaking family and individual therapy with children, young people and their families. Her research interests include domestic violence and the impact on children and young people's mental health, infant mental health and the mental health of young parents.

Rachel Barrell is a Principal Lecturer and Course Leader in Initial Teacher Education at the University of Worcester. She has been involved in primary education for over 20 years both in mainstream and special educational needs education. She has a strong interest in inclusive education, professional values and multi-professional practice. Rachel is also a National Teaching Fellow of the Higher Education Academy.

ACKNOWLEDGEMENTS

The authors would like to thank all of the students and practitioners who inspired and supported this text. Where necessary, case studies and examples used in the book have been adapted and anonymised.

1

MENTAL HEALTH AND EMOTIONAL WELL-BEING

Chapter objectives

By the end of this chapter you should be aware of:

- what we mean by 'whole school approach' in relation to the chapter;
- common mental health problems affecting children and young people;
- origins and prevalence;
- curiosity about changes in children and young people's behaviour;
- how changes in behaviour may be about a potential emerging mental health problem;
- the importance of getting a balance of not always pathologising children and young people's behaviour;
- how some presenting behaviours can be considered 'normal' when the context is understood, so the 'context' beyond the child may require attention;
- what contributes to poor mental health;
- treatments, interventions and therapeutic approaches;
- how schools can help.

Teachers' Standards

This chapter supports the development of the following Teachers' Standards:

TS8: Fulfil wider professional responsibilities

- Take responsibility for improving teaching through appropriate professional development, responding to advice and feedback from colleagues.
- Communicate effectively with parents with regard to pupils' achievements and well-being.

Introduction

The chapter will consider aspects of child and adolescent mental health with a brief overview of the most common presenting problems, together with consideration of the role schools, teaching and educational staff can play. Other important considerations in relation to child and adolescent mental health such as risk and resilience are explored in Chapter 4.

The 'No Health Without Mental Health' strategy (DoH, 2011) cited that over half of lifetime mental health problems begin to emerge by age 14, and three-quarters by the time people reach their mid-20s. Mental ill health really is a disease of the young at what should be an optimum time of life. These children and young people are often in our schools when their mental health problems are emerging. Mental health is the foundation of healthy development. Having mental health problems early in life can have adverse and long-lasting effects (Murphy and Fonagy, 2012). Teaching staff and other school staff are the professionals spending the most time with children and young people, more than any other professional group, and are well placed to notice any behaviour changes which may indicate a problem (Weare, 2015). School is a major part of children and young people's lives, as over a third of their time is spent in school – meeting and making friends there and with teaching staff playing a large part in their development (Royal College of Psychiatrists, 2016, p11). We have a 'window of opportunity' because of the progressing and continuing developmental aspects, unique to children and young people, for offering early help and support so that lifelong outcomes can be improved.

The Pursuit of Happiness report (CentreForum Commission, 2014, p36) and the House of Commons Health Committee (2014) recommends that teaching and educational staff should receive training in child development, mental health and psychological resilience so that vulnerable children can be identified. The CentreForum Commission recognised teachers are not mental health professionals but that they should have skills of recognition and know how to access help and when to refer to CAMHS. Other recommendations in the report include a requirement for the national curriculum to include teaching on children and young people's mental health and improving their resilience. The topic of child and adolescent mental health is now frequently featured in the media, and is the subject of frequent political debate. The most recent reports and events include 'Future in Mind: Promoting, protecting and improving our children and young people's mental health and well-being' (DoH, 2015). 'Future in Mind' is the findings and recommendations of the Children and Young People's Mental Health and Wellbeing Taskforce. It firmly sets a whole child and whole family approach, promoting good mental health at the earliest ages, and moving away from only thinking about mental health from a clinical position. It acknowledges the role schools are already playing in supporting pupil mental health and that this needs to be further developed by earlier identification of issues and early support.

Teaching children and young people how to improve their resilience should be a whole school approach with the promotion of emotional health and well-being embedded into the culture and core business of school settings. The report recommends promoting the emotional well-being of the whole school community, noted as very important given that educational staff have high rates of work related stress (CentreForum Commission, 2014, pp32–33; Weare, 2015). The MindEd e-portal was introduced in 2014 as an online electronic resource for professionals interested in child and adolescent mental health and provides clear guidance on children and young people's mental health, well-being and development. In 2017, Prime Minister Theresa May announced a commitment to improve mental health and well-being including Mental Health First Aid training for all secondary school staff with an additional emphasis on improving mental health in the workplace for staff (BACP, 2017).

Prevalence

The National Service Framework for Children, Young People and Maternity Services (2004) identified that 10 per cent of 5–15 year olds had a diagnosable mental health disorder. That is equivalent to an average of three children in every classroom in every school in Britain. A further 15 per cent have less severe problems and remain at an increased risk of future mental health problems (Brown et al., 2012, cited in Department for Education, 2015, p34). 'Future in Mind' (DoH, 2015) acknowledged that 1 in 10 children needs support for mental health problems. These figures are based on the B-CAMHS survey last commissioned and published over 13 years ago in 2004. There has been no full scale study since then. This has been criticised as now being long overdue by the Royal College of Paediatrics and Child Health (2014). Previously the study had been conducted every five years so there is now a lack of reliable up-to-date data (House of Commons Health Committee, 2014). Under 5s were not included in the 2004 survey despite the evidence for the importance of the early years as an opportunity for intervention. Research has suggested that between 50–60 per cent of children showing high levels of disruptive behaviour at 3–4 will continue to have these problems at school age (Murphy and Fonagy, 2012).

Understanding mental health in children and young people

Many mental health problems have their origins in childhood (Dogra et al., 2009). An accepted view is that mental health and ill health arises from a context of variables including biological factors such as genetics and brain development, and psychological variables that include coping mechanisms and how these then interact in relation to either adverse or positive environmental circumstances or experiences. Another way to consider this is that early experiences also impact on brain development, and it is the impact of these experiences on inherent temperament and character that psychological development therefore becomes influenced. An individual's inherent genes can be triggered by experiences in childhood. It is also important to consider and be mindful that most presenting mental health conditions are medicalised and are an interpretation of behaviours considered to be beyond what would be accepted as normal behaviour. But these can also be thought about from a psychological perspective. Often children and young people are 'acting out'. Acting out is a defence mechanism and defends the individual from anxiety and is an emotional and externally visible response to overwhelming and unmanageable feelings (Burton et al., 2014). It is important to try and understand the behaviour within the young person's context.

In relation to poor behaviour, approaches based on punishment focus on the negative and tend to be very common. For example practices such as writing the offending child's name on the classroom board for the day or withholding playtime in younger children do not get to the bottom of the problem. It is not helpful to come from a position that sees poor behaviour as intentional or under the child's control; bear in mind that usually it is not. Try and see the whole child behind the behaviour and instead of focusing on negatives, focus on positive characteristics (as discussed in Chapter 4) (Weare, 2015, p11). Incidentally, play is a right under Article 31 of the United Nations Convention on the Rights of the Child (1989) so there is really no case for withholding/rewarding using play in this way.

Very often, behaviours can be understood within their context and may be temporary and a reaction to adversity. For example a child may become anxious and not want to leave a parent and go to school. But if there are changed family circumstances such as bereavement, domestic abuse, or parental mental or physical illness this could explain the changed behaviour. That is not to say a clinical judgement is not required if a child is highly anxious or likely to be depressed, as it would be important to do so in order to access appropriate treatment. Using the term 'mental disorder' or 'problem' indicates that the issue resides within the child, and is not always helpful, but problems or disorders can develop as a reaction to external circumstances as shown by the case studies (Murphy and Fonagy, 2012). Similarly a diagnosis of 'attachment disorder' implies that there is something inherently wrong with the child. The reason a child has not been able to develop appropriate attachment, however, is a direct reflection of the impact of the adults'/primary caregivers' caring of the child (Dogra, 2011). One of the most important things to remember is when a change of behaviour is observed, be curious and explore what may be happening in the child or young person's context. We often make the mistake of expecting children and young people to 'behave' within what is considered 'normal' in the class and school settings but that can sometimes be an impossible task for a young person struggling to deal with any problems they may have or have encountered. If they feel misunderstood, criticised and ultimately unsafe it is likely to make things much worse for them.

Typical mental health problems in children and young people

Children and young people can experience the same mental health problems as adults. The difference between adults and children, which is important to understand, is the requirement to think about these presentations within the context of the developmental phase.

There is a considerable overlap across the range of problems and conditions, with an emotional element consistently present throughout. Some children may have both physical illness, with mental health problems or disorders as a combination or 'comorbidity'. For example, a young person with diabetes may place themselves at risk through non-compliance with diet and medication, which could be considered an aspect of self-harming behaviour. Overall children with mental health problems are also at increased risk of physical health problems (DoH, 2015, p25).

Presentations need to be thought of in the context of normal development which is on a continuum of constant change. It is important to remember that risk-taking behaviours and mood changes would be considered normal adolescent behaviour. Physical and hormonal changes leave the adolescent brain less able to regulate emotion and impulse (Weare, 2015). Not only do any potential symptoms need to be considered from a developmental perspective but also within the context of the child or young person and their experiences; therefore, what *is* and what *has* been happening (Burton et al., 2014).

The most common mental health problems for children and young people are depression, anxiety, conduct disorders, attention deficit hyperactivity disorder (ADHD), and autistic spectrum conditions (ASC) (Murphy and Fonagy, 2012). Other significant mental health conditions include: eating disorders such as anorexia nervosa, attachment disorder, post-traumatic stress disorder, self-harm, suicidal behaviours, mood changes, behaviour changes, relationship and attachment difficulties, substance misuse, changed eating patterns, isolation and social withdrawal and somatic problems. Somatising features and problems (physical symptoms with psychological origins) include, for example: headaches, enuresis and encopresis (faecal soiling), tummy aches and sleep disturbances, often present in younger children and can be fairly common with varying degrees of severity, frequency and persistence.

Depression

Depression is now recognised as a major public health problem in the UK and worldwide. It accounts for 15 per cent of all disability in high-income countries. In England, 1 in 6 adults and 1 in 20 children and young people at any one time are affected by depression and related conditions, such as anxiety. 0.9 per cent of children and young people are seriously depressed (DoH, 2015). According to the International Classification of Diseases (ICD-10) (World Health Organisation, 2010) and the Diagnostic Statistical Manual (DSM-5) (American Psychiatric Association, 2013), depression is characterised by an episodic disorder of varying degrees of severity characterised by depressed mood and loss of enjoyment persisting for several weeks. There must also be a presence of other symptoms including: depressive thinking; pessimism about future, suicidal ideas; and biological symptoms such as early waking, weight loss and reduced appetite (NICE, 2013a).

The criteria are similar for children and adults but with important differences (Keenan and Evans, 2009). With children and young people, developmental perspectives and context are highly relevant, as already discussed. For example, eating and sleeping disturbances often present as potential symptoms, but these would be common in childhood anyway. Tearfulness and crying has a very different meaning and incidence in childhood compared with adulthood. It is not uncommon to feel depressed at times. It is also important to 'normalise' sadness as a passing human condition. If sadness became persistent over time this would be different and a cause for concern (Burton et al., 2014).

Anxiety

Anxiety, it must be remembered, is normal. Anxiety becomes pathological when the fear is out of proportion to the context of the life situation and, in childhood, when it is out of keeping with the expected behaviour for the developmental stage of the child (Lask, 2003). It is also one of the most common mental health problems with an estimated 300,000 young people or 3.3 per cent in Britain having an anxiety disorder (Royal College of Psychiatrists, 2014; DoH, 2015). For example separation anxiety would be considered normal for infants (leaving a primary carer) but less so for a teenager. In a relatively short time span, in comparison to the full length of human life, children move from a state of limited emotional understanding to becoming complex individuals. The number and complexity of emotional experiences together with modulation of human expression increase with age. It is therefore not surprising that some children and young people are easily overwhelmed and experience emotional disorders, which if they persist are debilitating and require intervention and help. There are many variations of anxiety and children can experience anxiety in some of the following ways: worries, phobias, separation anxiety, panic disorder, post-traumatic stress disorder and obsessive compulsive disorder. Thinking about the above variations in how anxiety is expressed it is useful to consider a developmental perspective – there are different fears for different years. In infancy if secure attachment is accomplished, fear of separation from a caregiver diminishes. Separation anxiety usually begins in the pre-school years any time after the attachment period but typically in late childhood, early adolescence. Other fears, such as fear of the dark, can appear, and then, as the imagination develops, ghosts and monsters. Animal phobias, such as a fear of spiders or dogs, usually begin in childhood. Performance anxiety can emerge in late childhood and social anxiety in adolescence. Fears and anxieties are normal developmental challenges facing the maturing individual. During adolescence, autonomy and independence are major developmental challenges, endeavouring to balance between compliance with rules and expressing independent autonomy. It is normal to experience conflict to some level, but the challenge posed by emerging autonomy can trigger or exacerbate interpersonal problems that require negotiation with the accompanying anxiety (Burton et al., 2014; Royal College of Psychiatrists, 2014; Young Minds, 2016).

Conduct disorders

5.8 per cent of children and young people have a conduct disorder (DoH, 2015).

> *Conduct disorders nearly always have a significant impact on functioning and quality of life. The 1999 ONS survey demonstrated that conduct disorders have a steep social class gradient, with a three to fourfold increase in prevalence in social classes D and E compared with social class A. The 2004 survey found that almost 40 per cent of looked-after children, those who had been abused and those on child protection or safeguarding registers had a conduct disorder.*

(NICE, 2013b, p4)

Conduct disorder refers to aggressive, destructive and disruptive behaviours in childhood that are serious and likely to impair a child's development. In DSM-5 there is a distinction between oppositional defiant disorder (characterised by recurrent negativistic, defiant, disobedient and hostile behaviours) and conduct disorder, which includes a presence of repetitive persistent violations of societal norms and other people's basic rights. In ICD-10 oppositional and conduct problems are both included under the heading of conduct disorder. Many behaviours included in the diagnosis are common in normal child development, but when they are persistent and frequent they bring increased risks in later life including: anti-social behaviours, a range of psychiatric disorders, educational and work failure and relationship difficulties (Moffitt et al., 2002). Conduct disorder is more common in boys than girls (NICE, 2013b). There is frequently co-morbidity with other illness including substance misuse, anxiety and ADHD. It is considered there is substantial heritability but little is known about the mechanisms. Individual risk factors include low school achievement and impulsiveness; family risk factors include parental contact with the criminal justice system and child abuse; social risk factors include low family income and little education (NICE, 2013b).

Parenting practices in families of conduct-disordered children are reported as often hostile and critical, with harsh discipline, a lack of consistent rules, low monitoring of behaviours and parental disagreements. Un-cooperative behaviour and aggression is frequently cited as a reason for school exclusion. Often, these sorts of behavioural problems can be linked to communication difficulties. A research study by Gilmour et al. (2004) found that pragmatic difficulties underlie anti-social behaviour in a proportion of children diagnosed with conduct disorder. Many have deficits in pragmatic language skills in a similar way to children on the autistic spectrum. Significant numbers of children with autistic spectrum disorders remain undetected. The research further cited that children with such deficits do not tend to use language in a way that takes account of a social hierarchy (peer, teaching assistant, head teacher), and are unaware of the adverse consequences.

Where there is a combination of inherited vulnerability plus negative parenting, especially early negative affect and intrusive control, these factors contribute to the development and persistence of conduct problems. These are often highly vulnerable young people and can be at risk to themselves and others (Burton et al., 2014).

Attention deficit hyperactivity disorder (ADHD)

1.5 per cent of children and young people have severe ADHD (DoH, 2015). Characteristics of ADHD include a triad or constellation of impairments in the following three areas:

- Poor concentration.

- Hyperactivity.

- Impulsiveness.

It is important to recognise that displaying the above behaviours does not necessarily mean ADHD is the explanation. These behaviours may indicate psychological causes. Think about how you might behave if you were in a stressful situation, experiencing stress and anxiety – all of the above areas are likely to show changes. A key factor is the persistence and frequency in all domains (Burton et al., 2014).

A problem for children and young people is that their ADHD impairments can impact significantly on educational experiences and attainment. Young people with ADHD have a higher rate of behavioural and disruptive disorders and are disproportionately represented in the youth justice service. Children with ADHD struggle to regulate activity and they are not able to evaluate their responses beforehand or subsequently. Exhortations often made of them to 'try harder' or 'learn to concentrate' are impossible to fulfil, are unhelpful and tend to reinforce failure.

The range of possible lifetime impairment extends to educational and occupational underachievement, dangerous driving, difficulties in carrying out daily activities such as shopping and organising household tasks, in making and keeping friends, in intimate relationships (for example, excessive disagreement) and with childcare (NICE, 2008, p5).

As with other disorders ADHD is classified in both ICD-10 (hyperkinetic disorder) and in DSM-5. Severe ADHD corresponds approximately to the ICD-10 diagnosis of hyperkinetic disorder. This is defined as when hyperactivity, impulsivity and inattention are all present in multiple settings, and when impairment affects multiple domains in multiple settings. Part of the assessment process would include collecting information from parents and from educational settings. Diagnosis is a matter of clinical judgement which considers the severity of impairment, pervasiveness, individual factors and familial and social context (NICE, 2008).

There are strong genetic influences and often history-taking reveals other family members exhibiting ADHD traits that are undiagnosed; this is significantly so in earlier generations where ADHD was unrecognised. No single gene has yet been identified. Environmental factors include maternal drug and alcohol use in pregnancy. In addition, ongoing effects of individual and parental substance misuse, poor or hostile parenting also needs to be considered. In the UK, a survey of 10,438 children between the ages of 5 and 15 years found that 3.62 per cent of boys and 0.85 per cent of girls had ADHD (Ford et al., 2003). ADHD seems to be approximately four times more common in boys than girls.

It can be helpful to re-frame the negative symptoms of ADHD in terms of positive aspects. It is not always helpful to focus on reducing 'unwanted' behaviours; alternatively it is better to harness the positives (as discussed in Chapter 4). There is potential for these young people as they usually have energy and enthusiasm by the bucket load. They have a 'feet first' activist approach, which during childhood and adolescence can get you into trouble but needs to be seen as also having advantages. It can be difficult to 'fit in' to 'systems', however, especially the demands of education, which can be stacked against a child or young person with ADHD (Burton et al., 2014).

Autistic spectrum conditions (ASC)

Autism in Britain was first labelled as childhood psychosis at the beginning of the twentieth century. In 1944 it was named 'Kanners Syndrome', and then in the latter part of the twentieth century 'Autism' (Wing, 1996). Asperger's Syndrome was identified in 1944 although it took until 1979 for Asperger's work to be translated from German to English. It wasn't until 1991 that the term Asperger's Syndrome was recognised in Britain. The difference between autism and Asperger's syndrome is that 'Aspies' are of average or higher intelligence and develop language skills in the normal developmental way; the reverse is true for autistic people (Bradshaw, 2013, p55).

Autistic spectrum conditions or disorders form a very broad variation in presentation. 'Spectrum' indicates that while sharing the same condition there is a wide range of difficulties experienced in different ways. On a scale of 0–100 on the spectrum, a social and communicative person would appear at the starting point of the scale, zero. Moving further along the spectrum someone with a few autistic traits, such as a need for routine, would appear. The stronger the autistic traits the further along the spectrum, so at 100 there would be a person with no speech and limited responses to others (Muggleton, 2012, p31). There may also be accompanying learning disabilities. It is a lifelong condition and, unlike all the other conditions discussed in this chapter, it has a biological origin and is a disorder of development. In addition, it is also important to remember that autistic children, young people and adults often experience sensitivity to sounds, touch, tastes, smells, light or colours (The National Autistic Society, 2013).

Autism is characterised by a triad of features related to impairments of functioning in:

- social communication;

- social understanding;

- social imagination and play.

There are also accompanying and ritualistic stereotyped interests and behaviours. These are usually evident from infancy although they may not be recognised at that point. Play is often a pre-occupation with repetitive activities.

Again, as with children and young people with ADHD, it is helpful to consider positives for Asperger's children. Having a diagnosis does not in itself change anything but it can help parents and teachers to understand a child's needs and put in place supportive measures. Strengths can be in individual sports, for example. Another trait is honesty; never ask 'how do I look?' If you are not prepared for an honest response, do not ask if the truth is going to hurt! Similarly language needs to be straightforward; if you ask a young person with Aspergers (often referred to as 'Aspie') to 'hold your horses', i.e. slow down, or say 'it's raining cats and dogs', you will have a puzzled response wondering where exactly the horses, cats and dogs are.

Eating disorders

Eating disorders can develop in childhood or adolescence in keeping with other mental health disorders, becoming most frequent with an age of onset of between 15–35 years. Anorexia nervosa has a mortality rate which is twice the level of any other illness and has the highest death rate of any mental illness (Treasure and Alexander, 2013). Anorexia has always been considered a predominantly female disorder, borne out by the statistics; nevertheless, professionals also need to be mindful of the fact that boys and young men do develop anorexia. It is generally considered that eating disorders, as with other psychological disorders and mental illnesses, arise from a combination of biological/medical, psychological and social or environmental factors as discussed above. It is the articulation and inter-relation of these overlapping theories, together with risk and resilience factors, as a combination, which leads to understanding and interpreting the causes of eating disorders, and not a single application of a model (Burton, 2014). However, the case for being driven predominantly by the medical genetic origin is quite strong. More recent research suggests a strong genetic link and pre-disposition, and demonstrates that anorexia nervosa is not a lifestyle choice but rather an inherent gene which is most probably present and becomes vulnerable when exposed to other factors (Lask et al., 2012). Other factors would include psychological attributes with perfectionism implicated as both a risk and a maintaining factor (Fairburn, 2003; Wade and Tiggeman, 2013). Typically, young people with anorexia often have 'perfectionist' traits and can be academically high achievers. But they often have low self-esteem and find it difficult to express or externalise negative emotions (Dhakras, 2005). Media and societal attitudes towards thinness are often cited as 'reasons' but they are not reasons in isolation, and can act as contributing factors or triggers. Other pre-disposing factors centre on the negotiation of transitional points, for example the negotiation of adolescence in combination with an adverse life event such as bereavement, parental divorce or sexual abuse, together with an inherent psychological vulnerability (Burton, 2014).

Self-harm and suicidal behaviour

Self-harm and suicidal behaviour are emotional disorders on a similar continuum as they are both in response to stress. Self-harm tends to be about coping whereas suicidal behaviour can be associated with giving up or seen as a solution to overwhelming and intolerable feelings but not necessarily about wanting to die. Young people who self-harm are at a higher risk of suicide. The Royal College of Psychiatrists report (2014) highlighted the fact that patterns of self-harm are evolving with the explosion of digital communication. Unfortunately, self-harm is frequently stigmatised with individuals being described as 'attention-seeking'. This is unhelpful and it is important to maintain curiosity over why the young person may be expressing their feelings in such a way in order to be able to offer appropriate support. It is important to assess all episodes of self-harm individually in a person-centred and systemic way, as failure to do so can lead to individuals feeling misunderstood (NICE, 2004). If it remains hidden it can lead to guilt and shame which is often compounded by the negative reactions of others (Nixon, 2011). Young people are vulnerable to suicidal feelings. The risk is greater when they have mental health problems or behavioural disorders, misuse substances, or have family breakdown or mental health problems or suicide in the family (DoH, 2011). Adolescence is the most turbulent developmental period since infancy with the biggest challenges and changes in all areas of biological, psychological and social change. Pre-disposing vulnerabilities such as poor or adverse early experiences can be activated during the adolescent phase (Anderson, 2008). Triggers influencing self-harm and suicidal behaviour include: bullying, difficulties with parental and peer relationships, bereavement, earlier abusive experiences, difficulties with sexuality, problems with ethnicity, culture, religion, substance misuse and low self-esteem. Contextual triggers include adverse family circumstances, dysfunctional relationships, domestic violence, poverty, parental criminality, time in local authority care, frequent punishments and family transitions. All of the above become compounded by adolescent developmental pathology (Harrington, 2003).

Bell (2000) describes how the cause given is actually the trigger precipitating suicidal behaviour, but it will often be the reason given by the young person, their families, and even doctors and other clinical staff. Reasons given might include an argument with a close friend or family member, or failing exams. The notion of a trigger as an explanation often leads to a minimising of the level of seriousness surrounding the suicide attempt which is *never* about the stated reason. Rather, it is a rationalisation of the event rather than an explanation as it may be a frightening prospect for all concerned to consider serious mental disturbance. This is a very important point to bear in mind and is the key to understanding suicidal ideation. For example not all individuals who have arguments and fail exams make attempts on their lives, therefore those that do so for those reasons given are responding to a trigger (the argument, exam failure) to much deeper intolerable problems.

Suicide and suicidal ideation always takes place within the context of relationships which is the important challenge to explore and understand. Usage of triggers as an explanation can lead to collusion and denial of the seriousness of the event, not only by family members but clinical staff also, and therefore it is highly risky in itself not to take the attempt seriously. Suicide attempts should be taken seriously and must never be minimised by describing somewhat trivial reasons such as relationship disagreements or exam failure which are in fact the precipitating triggers (Burton, 2014). The difference in self-harming behaviour, as opposed to an intention to kill oneself, is that with self-harm the person is in touch with their body through the physical reality of pain. The skin becomes a medium for communication (Gardner, 2001). Physical pain is often easier to manage than emotional pain which, when inflicted, can change mood, which, in turn, can be habit-forming. Cutting releases endorphins into the system, providing a brief calming effect, combined with serotonin as a mood enhancer. It can therefore be seen as a form of relief. There can also be something about experiencing first aid 'patching up' and 'repairing' either by the individual or helpers, with these repairing acts experienced as therapeutic.

KEY REFLECTIONS

- It is estimated that three children in every classroom have a diagnosable mental health condition; these figures are based on research now over 12 years old. These statistics are not expected to have reversed.
- Half of lifetime mental health problems (excluding dementia) begin to emerge by age 14 and three-quarters by the mid-20s.
- Mental ill health arises from a context of variables: genetic biological factors (bio-medical) and psychological factors and how these articulate with lived experiences (psychosocial).
- When considering children and young people, potential symptoms need to be assessed from a developmental and contextual perspective; for example 'risk-taking' behaviour could be considered part of adolescent pathology and therefore normal.
- Children and young people can experience the same mental health problems as adults.

Interventions, strategies and therapeutic treatment approaches: how can schools help?

The Annual Report of the Chief Medical Officer 2012, *Our Children Deserve Better: Prevention Pays*, included a key message that service design should recognise the role, importance and potential of schools in fostering the development of resilience and opportunities for delivering interventions that can improve mental health (Murphy and Fonagy, 2012, p12). Child and adolescent mental health sits within a medical and psychological diagnostic model. Children and young people, as already identified, tend to receive a diagnosis if an assessment reveals this to be appropriate. This will be a primarily medical interpretation but the approach both to interpretation and treatment is one which considers all factors, including psychological and sociological. An appropriate treatment or intervention is then recommended according to the diagnosis. Freeth (2007, as cited in Prever, 2010, p57) argues that this model does not sit well with the 'person-centred' approach, although CAMHS workers do adopt a 'person-centred' approach where the focus is on relationship-building alongside the treatment or intervention. Regardless of what sort of approach is used, cognitive behavioural therapy, solution focused therapy, eye movement de-sensitisation re-processing (which is receiving more attention for the treatment of post-traumatic stress disorder in CAMHS

(NICE 2005; Tufnell, 2005)) or family therapy and family work, the point is not to primarily pathologise an individual according to a diagnosis, but to adopt a person-centred relationship approach.

The person-centred approach is the most widely known of the humanistic approaches developed by Carl Rogers in the 1950s. Rogers' core conditions of empathy, unconditional positive regard and congruence tend to underpin all approaches of therapy and are the mainstay of the therapeutic relationship and effective communication (Rogers, 1957). In CAMHS, as discussed previously, a person-centred approach also considers the child and young person in relation to their context of family. Similarly for teaching staff it is essential to consider the child or young person's context in order to assist with understanding of what may be happening. Whilst doing so it is very important to remain 'child-focused' and to be in a position that maintains and supports the child or young person from an appropriately developmental position. Whilst the family can sometimes be seen as part of the problem, it is important to avoid a blaming stance and to also see the family as a resource for change.

Interventions and therapeutic approaches in CAMHS Tiers Two–Four usually include: play therapy, art therapy, parent–infant psychotherapy, under-5s work, cognitive behaviour therapy, individual work, family work, parenting work and family therapy. There will often be a combination model of a psychological and pharmacological intervention and approaches as shown in the case studies below.

For conduct disorder, multi-dimensional treatment can include parent work and individual work. Psychosocial therapies are the main approach to conduct disorders involving close working with parents through parenting programmes and parent–child interaction therapy with the key feature being positive parenting (Murphy and Fonagy, 2012). It can be combined with risperidone (pharmacological approach) for a short period alongside other approaches as above (NICE, 2013b).

Treatment approaches for ADHD include a pharmacological approach as first line treatment (in conjunction with parenting and individual programmes) for ADHD using a prescribed psychostimulant (methylphenidate) (NICE, 2008). Medication can help children with concentration so has a valid use in supporting children in school settings. It can buy *thinking time* so impulsivity is reduced, and that does help significantly with concentration. It can help with symptom (triad of impairments) control, and does not remain in the system for more than a few hours. Treatment 'holidays' can be taken, so for example, the young person may not need to take medication at the weekend or in the school holidays. Management of ADHD includes parent and teacher training in behavioural techniques as well as individual support for the young person. A multi-faceted and multi-agency approach in the management of ADHD includes teacher training in behavioural techniques. There are, however, side effects including loss of appetite and difficulty getting to sleep (Burton et al., 2014).

In schools there is an emerging and promising evidence base for mindfulness, not just for children but also school staff. It provides an opportunity for implementation, adoption and embedding into the curriculum as part of a whole school approach to emotional health and well-being (Weare, 2015; CentreForum Commission, 2014). Other whole school approaches include 'circle time' for younger children. In addition, nurture groups, peer mentoring and buddy systems offer important opportunities to build on children and young people's resilience factors and therefore mitigate risk factors as discussed in Chapter 4.

Strategies for improving the mental health of children and young people can operate at multiple levels. A goal for teaching and school staff is to develop relationships and partnerships with local agencies who can provide specialist support through service partnerships. But it is recognised that this is against a backdrop of reductions in CAMHS budgets, mainly in the Tier One and Two early intervention services. This has led to higher thresholds for referrals to CAMHS, leaving children, young people and families not able to access services until their problem is severe. It is interesting to consider this would be completely unacceptable for childhood cancer services (CentreForum Commission, 2014, p34). An increase in the tiny 6 per cent CAMHS budget of the overall mental health budget is long overdue (House of Commons Health Committee, 2014, points 80 and 86). Some of the most effective school interventions have proved to be targeted mental health services (TaMHS) where early identification and support prevents problems escalating. Weare (2015) noted that often schools wait too long, not wishing to 'label' and often thinking children will 'grow out' of problems. Where possible working with local agencies and CAMHS brings education and health together to think about children and young people where and as soon as concerns are raised.

KEY REFLECTIONS

- Schools have potential and opportunities to mitigate children's mental health through whole school approaches being embedded into the curriculum. Examples of these include mindfulness, nurture groups, buddy and peer mentoring systems.
- It is essential to consider the child's context as this contributes to understanding.
- There are multiple treatment approaches including psychological and pharmacological support.
- Many approaches are primarily about working with parents.
- Try to make links with professionals in CAMHS for joined up working and wrap around support.

CASE STUDY: JOE

Joe has a diagnosis of ADHD. He is easily distracted and finds it difficult to concentrate for very long and is sometimes impulsive.

Joe is 7 and in a primary school class with 20 other boys and girls. The classroom is sunny and bright, with equipment, bookshelves and storage boxes all around the room. There are posters and pictures on the walls. The teacher has a whiteboard. All the children sit at tables which join each other in a group. There are 4 children to each group of tables. They are facing each other and not the teacher who is standing at the front of the class. There is a teaching assistant helping Joe with his task. Joe is colouring in letter shapes and then cutting them out to stick on a poster. While he is colouring he keeps looking around the classroom and shouts over to his friend on another table who waves back. Joe starts talking to the boy opposite him. The other children round the table are busy working and cutting out. He is trying to concentrate but finds it difficult to stay on task. The teaching assistant reminds Joe to keep on colouring and then she helps him with the scissors and cutting out a letter R. Joe manages to cut out a letter L for which he receives praise. At the end of the lesson Joe receives a gold star for working hard. He rushes outside at break and tears round the playground with the other boys.

Case study reflections

- Consider classroom layouts; for children like Joe it can be harder to concentrate when he is facing other children, not the class teacher.
- Joe is having great support from the class TA.
- Joe is praised and rewarded for staying on task which will have been difficult for him.
- Playtime is a really important opportunity to let off steam and play before the next class.
- Sometimes children like Joe, who end up finding it difficult to concentrate and get into trouble, have play curtailed or minutes deducted. This is not helpful and is counter-productive.
- It can be helpful to reframe potential negative characteristics and focus on positive aspects of ADHD, as in higher energy levels and 'up for anything' traits.

Integrating psychological care into Tier One universal settings such as schools can work as a pre-ventative and protective strategy. School-based counselling is an available and accessible form of psychological therapy for young people in the UK, with approximately 70,000–90,000 young people accessing services per year (BACP, 2013). 'Future in Mind' (DoH, 2015) suggests a whole child and family approach with a move away from thinking purely clinically about child mental health with an emphasis on prevention, early intervention and recovery and that this needs to be considered and implemented universally across settings. The Pursuit of Happiness report (CentreForum, 2014, p36) recommends that for children with less severe and emerging mental health problems, there should be greater accessibility to psychological therapies in schools and that the service could be provided by a practitioner with a CAMHS background. In secondary schools, young people should have routine access to a named CAMHS worker. School nurses can be an essential resource with a significant proportion of their workload consisting of supporting children and young people with emotional and psychological difficulties (Bohenkamp et al., 2015). They often, however, lack mental health training. This has been recognised by the Royal College of Nursing as an important issue and they have asked for country-wide standardised mental health training (Brown, 2015). School nurses are on the front line in terms of being a health professional accessible to young people in schools and are well placed to offer support and make links within their school community and staff and also with other professionals and CAMHS.

Counselling and psychotherapy for children and young people is very different from the traditional adult approaches and needs to be developmentally appropriate, individualised, flexible and creative. It needs to engage young people who are often reluctant to talk or find it difficult to recognise or understand their feelings. The young person's context or system also requires attention as they are inter-related and one cannot function in isolation from the other. Children and young people are usually one part of a wider family and are often relatively powerless to change their situation unless their family are supportive of the changes. Typically, a young person may be receiving age-appropriate support individually but ideally, and if possible, this would also be alongside parent and family work (Burton et al., 2014).

CASE STUDY: SARAH-JANE (WITH THANKS TO DR CLARE SMITH)

Sarah-Jane is 5. She started in reception class in September and is one of the older children, having had her 5th birthday in late September. It is now mid-February and Sarah-Jane's teacher, Miss Jennings, is becoming increasingly worried as, although S-J's school attendance has been very poor since she began school, it is getting worse. S-J's attendance has averaged about 50 per cent since the start of term. Her mother is very good at letting school know when S-J is off by phoning in the morning when she's going to miss school and always sends a note when S-J goes back to school. The reasons she gives for keeping S-J off sound genuine, but just seem to be very frequent (cold, cough, earache, sore throat etc.). Miss Jennings is especially concerned that S-J, who has always been very quiet, has become almost silent. S-J seems very withdrawn and doesn't play much with other children at school. She is becoming harder and harder to engage, although she seems to be an exceptionally polite girl who appears keen to please. During the last week, S-J has cried frequently at school, often over little things.

S-J lives with her mother, father and younger sister who is 3. Mum used to be a librarian but did not return to work after having S-J. Dad works installing telephone networks and commutes by train into a nearby city, walking to the station each day – a total commute of about 1½ hours each way door to door. Sometimes he works away from home for a week at a time. The family moved to this town so as to be within walking distance of Mum's work and a bit nearer Dad's workplace to shorten his commute, a year or so before S-J was born. Both sets of grandparents live in the town where S-J's parents used to live, about three quarters of an hour drive away. All the grandparents work full time, so the family has very little grandparental support. S-J's mum has a driving licence but doesn't like to drive.

S-J is always immaculately dressed for school. Her mum walks her to and from school every day, with her little sister in the push chair. S-J's teacher has noted that Mum is very quiet and tends not to chat with the other mothers in the playground.

Case study reflections

- There were several external factors affecting S-J.
- Miss Jennings realised that S-J was becoming more and more anxious because she was getting behind at school (her projects weren't as good as the other children's because she wasn't there enough to get on with them) and this worried S-J.

- She recognised that Mum was keeping S-J off because she (Mum) was anxious about sending S-J to school – and so not sending her – when she had even the slightest snuffle or hint of being even a tiny bit unwell.

- She realised that Mum's anxiety about S-J was partly because she had no local support networks and hadn't made friends amongst the other mothers, so was socially isolated.

- Miss Jennings discussed the situation with the other reception class teacher and made a plan to support the situation such as identifying a member of staff to support S-J to successfully integrate with her peers at playtime.

- They asked for Mum's help with hearing the children read in the 'other' reception class (not S-J's). They suggested she come into school whenever the 3-year-old was at nursery. They guessed that if Mum had a commitment to come into school then S-J would have to come into school, too, so she wouldn't miss as much school and would become more confident.

- The plan worked. Both S-J and her mother became more confident and their self-esteem grew. Both became less anxious. Mum helped more and more at school and started to talk a little with the other mothers in the playground.

CASE STUDY, DISRUPTIVE BEHAVIOUR EXAMPLE: JANEK (WITH THANKS TO DR CLARE SMITH)

Janek is 8. He is in Year 4 at a mainstream primary school. He lives with his mother, Ania, and his younger brother, Marius, who is 5. The family is Polish but have lived in the UK for about 7 years. They travel back to Poland every summer to see Ania's parents. Janek's and Marius's parents separated when the boys were 5 and 2 and they see their father, Osa, alternate weekends when they spend Sunday afternoon and have tea with him and his new partner, Lindsay (who is white British), who live in another town. Both boys seem to get on well with Dad and Lindsay and do lots of fun things with them, but get home very tired on Sunday night. They also behave quite aggressively both at home and at school on the Monday and Tuesday after the weekend when they've seen Dad.

Mum works part-time in a local greengrocer's and is able to drop the children off at school on her way to work and finishes work in time to collect them from the after-school club at 4.30 p.m. each day. She gets a discount on the fruit and vegetables in the store, so the children have a very healthy diet. Mum appears to be warm and caring. She has no problems with Janek's behaviour at home unless she tries to get him to do homework, which he resists strongly.

Janek has a large, red birthmark covering one cheek (called a port wine stain). The other children at school are used to it and don't comment on it or tease Janek about it.

Janek's teacher, Miss Freer, complains that Janek is very disruptive at school. He shouts out and disrupts the class, drawing attention to himself and making the other children laugh. This is

(Continued)

(Continued)

especially problematic during literacy lessons or when the children have to settle down to their writing. Miss Freer feels that Janek does everything he can to avoid tasks that require prolonged writing.

When the class are doing PE or sport, Janek is able to focus well. He can be quite responsible in these settings and likes to help the teacher by carrying equipment etc. He thrives on the praise he receives for his efforts.

In the playground, Janek gets on well with his peers. He usually plays football at playtime with a large group of friends. He's a good, popular player who doesn't hog the ball and is able to set up others to score goals.

Janek got on well at Beavers but can be a bit disruptive at Cubs (which he has only just started), though he is fine when they are doing activities outside.

Case study reflections

- Avoidance of writing task.
- Tired and aggressive after seeing Dad.
- A bit disruptive at Cubs.

Summary

Janek is an 8-year-old Polish boy who displays disruptive avoidant behaviour when he has to undertake effortful writing tasks. When not faced with such tasks he can behave with maturity. He can also be a little disruptive at Cubs which might be related to his avoidance of writing or might be due to issues around his facial birthmark. He is good at sport and gets on well with his peers. He appears to be well supported by his parents, though he only sees his father fortnightly for a few hours. Janek and his brother also behave quite aggressively for about two days after seeing their father, which may be related to tiredness after a busy day or the change in routine/structure (safeguarding issues were ruled out in this case).

- Plan: Discuss with staff involved (such as teacher, SENCo) to seek their opinions and feedback on your thoughts.
- Consider, with them, whether further assessment of Janek's writing difficulty would be helpful at this stage. (Sensory/motor/coordination problem = occupational therapist. Cognitive problem, for example, possible dyslexia = SENCo or educational psychologist.)
- Discuss your thoughts with Janek, Mum (and Dad if possible) so as to develop a collaborative plan with them.
- Think about: Would Janek be happy to have some extra help with writing tasks? See someone to find out more (assessment)?
- Think about: Would Dad be happy to have the boys on a Saturday instead?
- Think about: How would Janek or Mum feel about talking to the Cub Scout leader about possible issues with Janek's birthmark or with tasks involving writing when he's at Cubs?

Whatever issues children and young people exhibit, what would seem vital is that all interested parties work together to support an individual's future mental health and well-being. This will be facilitated by a whole school approach to mental health and well-being which involves its leaders, the voice of the child, the school's learning environment, the expertise of the settings professionals and a strong partnership with individuals' parents, carers and outside agencies. Such an approach must be seen as a pro-active response to provide timely support to any mental health or well-being issues as they may arise. This may, in turn, lead to the promotion of a continual drive to promote resilience within the children and young people in schools.

 KEY REFLECTIONS

- Why is it so important to be aware of the myriad of factors that influence an individual's mental health and well-being?
- How might common mental health problems originate, affect and manifest themselves in children and young people?
- Why is it important that professionals do not always pathologise children and young people's behaviour?
- How important is it to understand children and young people's context when thinking about their behaviour?
- How can treatments, interventions and therapeutic approaches help?
- What is the role and importance of schools in supporting the needs of children and young people who exhibit mental health and well-being issues?

CHAPTER SUMMARY

- Problems often start in response to external factors around the child and not from within the child.
- Acting out and unwanted behaviours can be a coping mechanism and a way of hiding the hurt.
- Where early help and recognition is available, very often at school, problems can be mitigated and outcomes improved.
- Any change in behaviour provides a clue something may not be quite right and should initiate curiosity and further exploration as seen from the case studies.
- It is really helpful for school staff to see beyond the behaviour at what may be driving it.
- Focusing on positive aspects is the way forward as focusing on negative aspects through punishment is often counterproductive.
- Ideally schools and health especially CAMHS, where they are involved, should be thinking and working together to improve children's mental health and well-being both with individual cases and as a whole school approach.

── FURTHER READING ─────────────

How healthy behaviour supports children's wellbeing. Available at: www.gov.uk/government/uploads/system/uploads/attachment_data/file/232978/Smart_Restart_280813_web.pdf (accessed January 2017).

Geopel, J., Childerhouse, H. and Sharpe, S. (2015) *A Critical Approach to Equality and Special Needs and Disability: Inclusive Primary Teaching*. Northwich: Critical Publishing.

Geopel, J., Childerhouse, H. and Sharpe, S. (2015) *Primary Inclusion and the National Priorities: Key Extracts from Primary Inclusive Teaching*. Northwich: Critical Publishing.

── REFERENCES ─────────────

American Psychiatric Association (2013) Diagnostic Statistical Manual (5). Available at: http://psychiatry.org/psychiatrists/practice/dsm (accessed January 2017).

Anderson, R. (2008) A psychoanalytic approach to suicide in adolescents, in Briggs, S., Lemma, A. and Crouch W. (eds) *Relating to Self-Harm and Suicide Psychoanalytic Perspectives on Practice, Theory and Prevention*. East Sussex: Routledge.

Bell, D. (2000) Who is killing what or whom? Some notes on the internal phenomenology of suicide. *Psychoanalytic Psychotherapy*, 15(1): 21–37.

Bohenkamp, J.H., Stephan, S.H. and Bobo, N. (2015) Supporting student mental health: The role of the school nurse in co-ordinated school mental health care. *Psychology in the Schools*, 52(7): 714–727.

Bradshaw, S. (2013) *Asperger's Syndrome – That Explains Everything: Strategies for Education, Life and Just About Everything Else*. London: Jessica Kingsley.

British Association for Counselling and Psychotherapy (BACP) (2013) *School-based counselling: What is it and why we need it*. Available at: www.bacp.co.uk/admin/structure/files/pdf/11791_sbc_may2013.pdf (accessed January 2017).

British Association for Counselling and Psychotherapy (2017*) BACP welcomes PM speech on mental health and shared society*. Available at: www.bacp.co.uk/media/?newsId=4017 (accessed January 2017).

Brown, E.R. et al. (2012) cited in: Department for Education (2015) *Mental health and behaviour in schools: 34*. Available at: www.gov.uk/government/uploads/system/uploads/attachment_data/file/416786/Mental_Health_and_Behaviour_-_Information_and_Tools_for_Schools_240515.pdf (accessed January 2017).

Brown, J. (2015) School nurses need better mental health training. *Children and Young People Now*. Available at: www.cypnow.co.uk/cyp/news/1153192/school-nurses- per centE2 per cent80 per cent-98need-better-mental-health-training per centE2 per cent80 per cent99 (accessed January 2017).

Burton, M. (2014) Understanding eating disorders in young people. *Practice Nurse*, 25(12): 606–610.

Burton, M., Pavord, E. and Williams, B. (2014) *An Introduction to Child and Adolescent Mental Health*. London: SAGE.

CentreForum Commission (2014) *The pursuit of happiness: A new ambition for our mental health.* Available at: www.centreforum.org/assets/pubs/the-pursuit-of-happiness.pdf (accessed January 2017).

Department of Health (DoH) (2011) *No health without mental health: A cross government mental health outcomes strategy for people of all ages.* Available at: www.gov.uk/government/uploads/system/uploads/attachment_data/file/213761/dh_124058.pdf (accessed January 2017).

Department of Health (2015) *Future in mind: Promoting, protecting and improving our children and young people's mental health and wellbeing.* Available at: www.gov.uk/government/uploads/system/uploads/attachment_data/file/414024/Childrens_Mental_Health.pdf (accessed January 2017).

Dhakras, S. (2005) Anorexia nervosa, in Cooper, M., Hooper, C. and Thompson, M. (eds) *Child and Adolescent Mental Health Theory and Practice.* London: Hodder-Arnold, 156–163.

Dogra, N. (2011) Psychiatry by ten teachers, in Dogra, N., Lunn, B. and Cooper, S. (eds) *Disorders of Childhood and Adolescence.* London: Hodder & Soughton.

Dogra, N., Parkin, A., Gale, F. and Frake, C. (2009) *A Multidisciplinary Handbook of Child and Adolescent Mental Health for Front-line Professionals,* 2nd ed. London: Jessica Kingsley.

Fairburn, C.G. and Harrison, P. (2003) Eating disorders. *The Lancet,* 361: 407–416.

Ford, T., Goodman, R. and Meltzer, H. (2003) cited in: National Collaborating Centre for Mental Health (2009) *ADHD: The NICE Guideline on Diagnosis and Management of ADHD in Children, Young People and Adults.* London: The British Psychological Society and The Royal College of Psychiatrists, 26.

Freeth, R. (2007) cited in: Prever, M. (2010) *Counselling and Supporting Children and Young People: A Person-Centred Approach.* London: SAGE, 57.

Gardner, F. (2001) *Self-Harm: A Psychotherapeutic Approach.* East Sussex: Routledge.

Gilmour, J., Hill, B., Place, M. and Skuse, D.H. (2004) Social communication deficits in conduct disorder: A clinical and community survey. *The Journal of Child Psychology and Psychiatry,* 45(5): 967–978.

Harrington, R. (2003) Depression and suicidal behaviour, in Skuse, D.H. (ed.) *Child Psychology and Psychiatry: An Introduction.* Oxford: The Medicine Publishing Co, 125–128.

House of Commons Health Committee (2014) *Children's and adolescents' mental health and CAMHS, Third Report of Session 2014–15.* Available at: www.publications.parliament.uk/pa/cm201415/cmselect/cmhealth/342/342.pdf (accessed January 2017).

Keenan, T. and Evans, S. (2009) *An Introduction to Child Development.* London: SAGE.

Lask, B. (2003) *Practical Child Psychiatry: The Clinicians Guide.* London: BMJ Publishing Group.

Lask, B., Frampton, I. and Nunn, K. (2012) Anorexia nervosa: A noradrenergic dysregulation hypothesis. *Medical Hypotheses,* 78(5): 580–584.

Moffitt, T.E., Caspi, A., Harrington, H. and Milne, B.J. (2002) Males on the life-course-persistent and adolescence-limited antisocial pathways: Follow up at age 26. *Developmental Psychopathology,* 14: 179–207.

Muggleton, J. (2012) *Raising Martians from Crash Landing to Leaving Home: How to Help a Child with Asperger Syndrome or High-Functioning Autism.* London: Jessica Kingsley.

Murphy, M. and Fonagy, P. (2012) Mental health problems in children and young people, in Annual Report of the Chief Medical Officer (2012) *Our children deserve better: Prevention pays*. Available at: www. gov.uk/government/uploads/system/uploads/attachment_data/file/252660/33571_2901304_CMO_ Chapter_10.pdf (accessed January 2017).

National Service Framework (2004) *Children, young people and maternity services: The mental health and psychological wellbeing of children and young people*. Standard 9. Available at: www.gov.uk/government/ uploads/system/uploads/attachment_data/file/199959/National_Service_Framework_for_Children_ Young_People_and_Maternity_Services_-_The_Mental_Health__and_Psychological_Well-being_of_ Children_and_Young_People.pdf (accessed January 2017).

National Institute for Clinical Excellence (NICE) (2004) *Self-harm: The short-term physical and psychological management and secondary prevention of self-harm in primary and secondary care*. Available at: www.nice.org.uk/guidance/cg16/evidence/cg16-selfharm-full-guideline-2 (accessed January 2017).

National Institute for Clinical Excellence (2005) *Post-traumatic stress disorder (PTSD): The management of PTSD in adults and children in primary and secondary care*. Available at: http://assisttraumacare.org.uk/ wp-content/uploads/NICE-PTSD-Quick-Ref-CG026.pdf (accessed January 2017).

National Institute for Clinical Excellence (2008) *Attention deficit hyperactivity disorder: Diagnosis and management of ADHD in children, young people and adults*. Available at: www.nice.org.uk/nicemedia/ live/12061/42059/42059.pdf (accessed January 2017).

National Institute for Clinical Excellence (2013a) *Depression in children and young people,* Quality standard QS48. Available at: www.nice.org.uk/guidance/qs48 (accessed January 2017).

National Institute for Clinical Excellence (2013b) *Antisocial behaviour and conduct disorder in children and young people: Recognition and management*. Available at: https://www.nice.org.uk/guidance/cg158/ resources/antisocial-behaviour-and-conduct-disorders-in-children-and-young-people-recognition- and-management-35109638019781 (accessed January 2017).

Nixon, B. (2011) *Self-harm in Children and Young People Handbook*. National CAMHS Support Service, National Workforce Programme. Available at: www.chimat.org.uk/resource/item.aspx?RID=105602 (accessed March 2017).

Prever, M. (2010) *Counselling and Supporting Children and Young People: A Person-centred Approach*. London: SAGE.

Rogers, C. (1957) The necessary and sufficient conditions for therapeutic change. *Journal of Consulting Psychology*, 21: 95–103.

Royal College of Paediatrics and Child Health (2014) *Making the UK's child health outcomes comparable to the best in the world: A vision for 2015*. Available at: www.rcpch.ac.uk/system/files/protected/news/ RCPCH per cent20Child per cent20Health per cent20Manifesto per cent20WEB.pdf (accessed January 2017).

Royal College of Psychiatrists (2014) *Worries and anxieties – helping children to cope: Information for parents, carers and anyone who works with young people*. Mental health and growing up factsheet. Available at: www.rcpsych.ac.uk/healthadvice/parentsandyouthinfo/parentscarers/worriesandanxieties.aspx (accessed January 2017).

Royal College of Psychiatrists (2016) *Values-based child and adolescent mental health system commission: What really matters in children and young people's mental health.* Available at: www.rcpsych.ac.uk/pdf/ Values-based per cent20full per cent20report.pdf (accessed January 2017).

The National Autistic Society (2013) *What is autism?* Available at: www.autism.org.uk/about-autism/ autism-and-asperger-syndrome-an-introduction/what-is-autism.aspx (accessed January 2017).

Treasure, J. and Alexander, J. (2013) *Anorexia Nervosa: A Recovery Guide for Sufferers, Families and Friends.* London: Routledge.

Tufnell, G. (2005) Eye movement desensitization and reprocessing in the treatment of pre-adolescent children with post-traumatic symptoms. *Clinical Child Psychology and Psychiatry,* 10(4): 587–600.

United Nations Convention on the Rights of the Child (1989) Article 31, Right to Play. Available at: http://353ld710iigr2n4po7k4kgvv-wpengine.netdna-ssl.com/wp-content/uploads/2010/05/UNCRC_ PRESS200910web.pdf (accessed January 2017).

Wade, T.D. and Tiggeman, M. (2013) The role of perfectionism in body dissatisfaction. *Journal of Eating Disorders.* Available at: https://jeatdisord.biomedcentral.com/articles/10.1186/2050-2974-1-2 (accessed January 2017).

Weare, K. (2015) *What Works in Promoting Social and Emotional Well-being and Responding to Mental Health Problems in School?* London: National Children's Bureau.

Wing, L. (1996) *The Autistic Spectrum.* London: Constable.

World Health Organisation (2010) International Classification of Diseases (ICD-10). Available at: www.who.int/classifications/icd/en/ (accessed January 2017).

Young Minds (2016) *About anxiety.* Available at: www.youngminds.org.uk/for_parents/worried_about_ your_child/anxiety/dealing_anxiety (accessed January 2017).

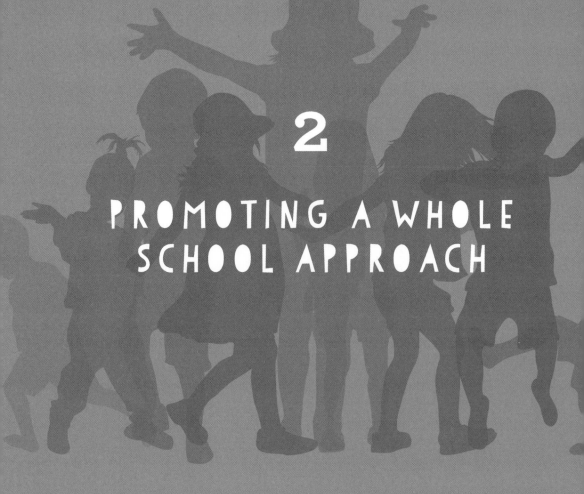

2
PROMOTING A WHOLE
SCHOOL APPROACH

Chapter objectives

By the end of this chapter you should be aware of:

- the rationale behind a whole school approach to mental health and well-being;
- why and how the leadership and management of a school should promote such an approach;
- the importance of the school's ethos, culture, curriculum, practice and environment in promoting a unified approach to mental health and well-being;
- the role of children and young people in providing a voice to inform and support change;
- how continuing professional development underpins the successful whole school approach;
- how a partnership between parents, carers and outside agencies is vital in supporting whole school mental health and well-being.

Teachers' Standards

This chapter supports the development of the following Teachers' Standards:

TS8: Fulfil wider professional responsibilities

- Take responsibility for improving teaching through appropriate professional development, responding to advice and feedback from colleagues.
- Communicate effectively with parents with regard to pupils' achievements and well-being.

Part Two: Personal and professional conduct

- Having regard for the need to safeguard pupils' well-being, in accordance with statutory provisions.
- Teachers must have proper and professional regard for the ethos, policies and practices of the school in which they teach.
- Teachers must have an understanding of, and always act within, the statutory frameworks which set out their professional duties and responsibilities.

Introduction

This chapter will focus on the need for a whole school approach to mental health and well-being. It will examine the role that the leadership and management of a setting can play in promoting a clear, agreed policy to underpin such an approach. It will examine how the establishment of such a policy may serve to inform and therefore to pervade the life of the school. This may be seen in terms of the setting's ethos, culture, learning environment, curriculum and professional practice. The role of children and young people and their voice will be considered with regard to the important part it can play in establishing, informing and underpinning such a whole school approach. Finally the role of teachers' continuing professional development will be considered as a means of enhancing practice. Alongside this, the partnership between parents, carers and outside agencies will be outlined for the vital role it plays in supporting a whole school approach to mental health and well-being.

Why is a whole school approach to mental health and well-being needed?

As children and young people move through their schooling, hormonal and physiological changes will inevitably lead to variations in expression of emotions and feelings. Given such changes it could be argued that such an all-pervading whole school approach to mental health and well-being is vital, as children and young people will be learning how to recognise and manage the ebbing and flowing of emotions as a result of the maturation process. A whole school approach to mental health and well-being may therefore be seen as a pro-active, progressive response to provide a timely response to any mental health or well-being issues as they may arise. This in turn may promote a school's continual drive to promote resilience within the children and young people in their care. Schools can promote resilience to mental health issues by

> *providing pupils with inner resources that they can draw on as a buffer when negative or stressful things happen.*

> (DfE, 2016, p19)

For some children and young people who face additional challenges at home and within their families, a whole school approach, providing support for them when it is needed, can offer an important role in an individual's life (Weare and Nind, 2011). Schools can provide a 'protective health asset', which can thus provide children and young people with a positive identity and learning opportunities as well as the skills needed to mediate against life's challenges (Brooks, 2012, p6). A whole school approach to mental health and well-being can also serve to help children and young people navigate through, and become more resilient towards, the range of their many social pressures. As well as peer relationships, this may include their use of social media, which may lead to unwanted peer pressure through activities such as cyberbullying. Such activities must be seen as a growing concern for individuals. In research by NCB and ASCL (Newson, 2016; NCB/ASCL, 2016) school leaders reported that over 40 per cent of young people indicated a large problem centred on cyberbullying, with nearly eight out of ten individuals (79 per cent) reporting an increase in self-harm or suicidal thoughts. Given this, it would seem vital that schools remain vigilant and respond in a proactive, timely, whole school manner to the myriad of life's challenges that may now affect the mental health and well-being of children and young people.

A whole school approach to mental health and well-being is not meant to provide a substitute to specialised clinical support. However, it should serve to complement the many items that teachers can do to support children and young people with school-based strategies, providing a holistic drive to support the prevention and deterioration of mental health and well-being. Stirling and Emery (2016) note that often a focus on mental health and well-being can be seen as a distraction for schools given the pressure placed on them by budgets, the curriculum and the standards agenda. However, given the current government guidance (DfE, 2016) which signals the vital importance of looking at mental health as part of an effective educational provision and as a means to support-ing the 'whole child' within their care, its place in school based provision cannot be ignored. For as Stirling and Emery (2016) note, if done well, not only can attainment be raised and enhanced but it may also lead to a reduction in exclusions and positive relationships which may lead to the attrac-tion and retention of school staff.

Schools can play an important role in the central social positioning of children and young people's development. As Cowie et al. (2004) suggest, individuals' relationships with their peers in schools can be crucial in supporting emotional well-being. Educational settings should pro-mote healthy, positive peer relationships, as well as supporting those isolated or withdrawn due to factors such as bullying. The Department of Health (2015) suggests that due to their position in children and young people's lives, schools fit well with what may be seen as a universal services-led approach. Their positioning not only promotes, but also leads, prevention-based activities linked to delivering and supporting the mental health and well-being of children and young people (DoH, 2015).

Many reports, such as Brooks (2012) and Public Health (2015), clearly indicate that the implementa-tion of a whole school approach to mental health and well-being, if applied consistently, not only has a positive impact in promoting a child/young person's physical health and mental well-being but also can serve to prevent mental health problems from arising or developing further. However, Weare (2015, p6) cautions against what can be seen sometimes as 'vague and diluted' approaches. It is important to remember that despite the valuable role that schools can play in promoting and supporting individuals who themselves have developed mental health and well-being issues linked to factors outside of school, such settings themselves may in turn lead unwittingly to unwanted personal well-being issues through poor attainment or through moments of school or secondary transition (Brooks, 2012). As Banerjee et al. (2016, p11) note:

> school-based experiences of being bullied or socially excluded, of damaging instructional and assess-ment practices and of repeated and chronic school failure can potentially have long-lasting impacts upon later well-being.

Thus, given the significant role that schools can often play in the development of the health and well-being of individuals, they have a duty to support individuals in their own trajectories whatever the personal journey such children and young people are on. Wyn et al. (2000) suggest such work is part of schools' core business. Such ideals would seem to be shared by our inspection regime given that Ofsted have placed such a focus in their Inspection Framework (Ofsted, 2015) when judging the quality of leadership and management with regard to schools seeking to overcome barriers for learning. By monitoring the provision and actions of the school and by scrutinising a range of records such as that of bullying, racism and homophobia incidents, Ofsted (2015, p51) will be able to be informed of how well a school provision not only contributes to the physical safety of children and young people but also in regard to their 'emotional health, safety and well-being'. 'Outstanding' schools will ensure that the interaction and interplay between families and such settings create environments where

> *children make consistently high rates of progress in relation to their starting points and are extremely well prepared academically, socially and emotionally for the next stage of their education.*

> (Ofsted, 2015, p75)

However, Weare (2015) cautions that despite our best effort, without identification and support the mental health and well-being problems of children and young people will not go away. This is a result of the many encountered problems being multiple and often going undetected in schools.

 **KEY REFLECTIONS**

- Why is a whole school approach to mental health and well-being vital to success for a school's children and young people?
- How might such a whole school approach fit in with a school improvement agenda?

A whole school approach to mental health and well-being

With reports such as Public Health England (2015) indicating the worrying levels of children who are currently suffering from mental health and well-being issues, it would seem more important than ever that a concerted effort is made by schools to support children and young people who are affected by such issues. Not only is it their duty to do their very best for all children and young people in their care, but also it would seem vital that a whole school approach to mental health and well-being should be placed at the very centre of the life and practices of a school. By taking such a macro, whole school approach, and by creating a shared ethos for the practical implementation of such ideals and practices, effective support mechanisms may be established for those at risk with mental health and well-being issues in our educational settings. This macro-commitment is of importance if such an approach wishes to be all-pervading in the setting, filtering down to the best of class-based practice as well as creating a culture of belonging for individuals. All elements of this approach and practice should be nourished by the voice of the child and young person, through the support and relationships offered and by the school's commitment to all staff's continued professional

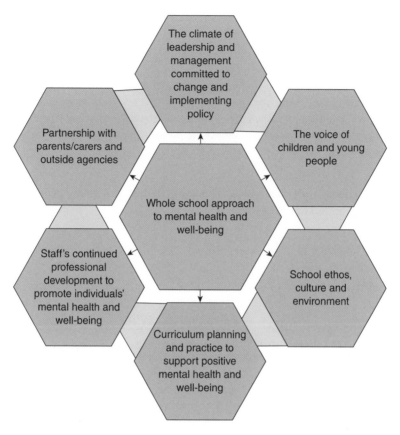

Figure 2.1 A whole school approach to mental health and well-being

development to support such a focus. As Weare (2015) concludes it is important for schools to begin with a central universal focus on positive well-being. Such a collective universal approach promotes the development of a culture where mental health and well-being is seen as the norm that allows for emotions and feelings to be discussed, where asking for help is fine in a non-stigmatising environment and where the attitudes and skill base of individuals can provide support when needed.

Figure 2.1 illustrates the central role that a whole school approach to mental health and well-being should play in school life as well as the contributory factors needed to maximise the effectiveness of such an approach.

Leadership and management

Leadership and management is central to any effective strategy in schools, holding a strategic position in a school's development as well as being pivotal in planning for, and bringing about, whole school change centred on a coherent whole school policy for mental health and well-being. Such a whole school policy provides the basis for a climate which challenges and prevents any stigma attached to mental health and well-being issues.

It is important to note that though the school's mental health and well-being policy may outline a school's position on the topic, as well as outlining its many practices, it should not sit in isolation from other school policies. It is not just important that any agreed actions are 'integrated, sustained and monitored' but also that

> a commitment to addressing social and emotional wellbeing is referenced within improvement plans, policies (such as safeguarding; confidentiality; personal, social, health and economic (PSHE) education; social, moral, spiritual and cultural (SMSC) education; behaviour and rewards) and practice.

(Public Health England, 2015, p7)

Other aspects of a school's work that may also support children and young people in this aspect of their lives may also be found in policies such as:

* drug education;

* inclusion;

* anti-bullying;

* attendance.

School leaders also need to acknowledge that for a whole school approach to mental health and well-being to be effective the outlining of policy alone is not enough. For any approach to be effective it must encompass the 'whole school' and avoid focusing on disconnected singular approaches. Weare (2015, p5) suggests that in order for schools to have an effective whole school approach to promoting well-being and mental health issues it must be seen in terms of being a coherent 'multi-component approach' which uses and encompasses the full potential of the entirety of a school's experience. Weare (2015, p5) also goes on to note that a whole school approach to mental health and well-being should be *everyone's business, with genuine involvement of all staff, pupils, governors, parents and the community and outside agencies.*

However, before any such whole approach can become effective in any setting, as Stirling and Emery (2016) suggest, it has to be based around the establishment of what may be seen as a shared understanding and commitment for such a focus. If such a policy is to be shared and owned by stakeholders then it is vital that all members of staff alongside the wider community of the school are involved in its establishment. This must start with a shared and agreed definition of what social and emotional well-being and mental health means in the setting. As Stirling and Emery (2016, p5) note:

> a shared understanding of the language you use in your school about social and emotional wellbeing and mental health problems helps clear and consistent conversations internally with staff and students with external services, parents and carers.

So how does a school go about developing such a process? Such an approach is outlined by Stirling and Emery (2016) in their self-assessment and improvement tool for school leaders. In this document Stirling and Emery outline several key questions and activities that you should consider when promoting a dialogue around a shared language (if this is not already the case) and a commitment to change and development. These include:

- What is your consistently understood definition for social and emotional well-being for individuals, children and young people in your setting?

- Where you hold differing views, do they centre on interpretation?

- When you share agreed ideas, what are the key priorities and are there any actions needed?

- If items are not accepted or understood, try and ascertain why this is currently the case.

- How might the evidence base inform your practice?

- What universal and targeted approaches work for you and which cause concern?

- Identify what mental health needs do individuals have in your setting and are there issues that you are currently avoiding?

- What individuals or group will lead and implement this change, be accountable for it and prioritise this approach and its actions?

- How are children,young people, parents/carers and external partners given a voice in this process in your setting?

(Stirling and Emery, 2016)

It is important to remember that support for the senior leadership is vital if such work is to be acknowledged and embedded within any setting (Public Health England, 2015). This may be achieved by having a knowledgeable and sympathetic governor who is able to champion mental health and well-being issues. Alternatively, such a role may also be found outside that of senior management just as long as the individual has the support of the leadership, management and governors of the school (Public Health England, 2015). Further to this, as the Department of Health (2015, p52) suggests, schools should think about creating a named lead for mental health issues to promote effective liaison between other support agencies such as GP practices.

For any policy to be effective it must remain current and reflect the evolving needs of each setting. Therefore once a school's leadership and management team have created such a policy it must be reviewed regularly, be seen as being 'live' and be capable of responding to the ongoing needs of each setting (Public Health England, 2015).

 KEY REFLECTIONS

- How might a mental health and well-being policy support a successful approach to this focus?
- What steps might the leadership and management take to establish such a policy?
- Why must all stakeholders be involved in its establishment?

The school ethos, culture and environment

Once the leadership and management team have led a whole school community through the process of engaging in and establishing the values that underpin a whole school policy for mental health and well-being, the agreed commitment may permeate the life and practice of the school through its culture and ethos. In a successful inclusive school's ethos, co-operation between all parties will be seen as the norm, with the voice of the individual being heard, with colleagues taking a collegiate approach towards one another (Cole, 2015). The ethos of a school, as Weare (2015) suggests, provides a tone which is all pervading throughout the setting. It provides a context in which children feel secure, know they are valued as individuals, are safe from emotional and physical harm and are able to discuss their interests and voice their fears in a supportive atmosphere (Ofsted, 2005). A supportive and positive school ethos will, as Weare (2015) rightly acknowledges, allow for a feeling of acceptance, that of being respected, and the creation of strong bonds between individuals and their settings. This may ultimately lead to low levels of conflict, respectful communications, appropriate expression of emotions and an environment which is responsive to individual needs (Weare, 2015).

A supportive, safe and positive ethos for mental health and well-being will no doubt manifest itself through the school's culture of an open door policy, through staff who are approachable and through its use of nurture groups and quiet areas or rooms in the school. There will be clearly identified individuals who children and young people can approach if worried or concerned. It will forge a school where diversity is celebrated and accepted. Strategies to support the mental health and well-being of its children and young people at classroom level will seek to develop an individual's sense of self-esteem. This could include having an individual's personal strengths celebrated by use of class-based rewards systems or items such as 'star of the day'. The classroom can also present a supportive and safe environment in which children can discuss and develop areas of low self-confidence or self-esteem through the use of PSHE-based strategies and practices such as circle time or items such as 'worry boxes'. The culture that has been created will mean that relationships between the teacher and the children and young people will be positive. This is important, as

> the social environment in which staff and pupils spend a high proportion of each weekday may have a profound effect on their physical, emotional and mental health.
>
> (Public Health, 2012, p7)

It is important to realise that in schools it is not only the school ethos and culture which is of significance but also that of the whole school environment including the teaching and learning opportunities provided. You may wish to consider whether your school offers the following:

* A school environment which allows for quiet areas as well as areas to promote play to support the range of individual needs?

* A respectful school and classroom environment which allows all pupils to feel safe and valued?

* School grounds and toilet areas which make it harder for young children to be intimidated or bullied out of sight?

- A school building which promotes a positive sense of mood by its quality of decoration and display?

- A staffroom which provides a quiet, comfortable place away from the pressures of the school day for staff?

KEY REFLECTIONS

- Why is a school's ethos and culture so valuable in supporting a climate that supports mental health and well-being?
- How might the wider school environment support individuals' emotional well-being?

Curriculum planning and practice

Surely one of the key roles that the planning and delivery of curricular items in schools can have in promoting resilience with regard to mental health and well-being is that of promoting emotional intelligence within children and young people. As Weare (2015, p10) suggests:

skills are not acquired by osmosis, they involve the school taking a conscious, planned and explicit approach through the taught curriculum.

Many opportunities can be provided by each setting to promote and develop social and emotional skills not only through their use of personal, social, health and economic education (PSHE) and their social, moral, spiritual and cultural (SMSC) provision, but also through the wider curriculum in general.

This may include, for example:

- Physical education, where structured activities can promote the feelings of positive self-esteem through items such as leadership as well as teaching the value of co-operation and teamwork.

- Music, art and design, where a variety of media are used to explore feelings and emotions.

- Literacy, where fiction, non-fiction and a range of writing genres can be explored, promoted and linked to life issues (such as in the novel *The Story of Tracey Beaker* by Jaqueline Wilson).

- Religious education, which promotes an exploration of items such as spirituality.

SMSC is seen by Ofsted (2015) as an important aspect of an individual's development. It may be seen to pervade the life of the school both in many aspects of the taught curriculum such as cultural development through religious education but also through opportunities such as circle time which allows children and young people to develop the knowledge, skill and understanding that may underpin their social, moral and spiritual development. As children grow into young people SMSC may be seen to manifest itself in terms of a 'citizenship curriculum'. This forms part of the Key Stage 3 and 4 curriculum which serves to ensure that an individual can form part of an important and valued part of society whatever their contribution can be.

Given that PSHE is a non-statutory part of the national curriculum (DfE, 2013), settings may freely interpret its delivery and content so that it may complement and enhance the statutory content of the national curriculum (DfE, 2014). Though PSHE may support the school's own curriculum, it can be linked to other statutory guidance on mental health and well-being, including drug education, sex and relationship education (SRE) and that of physical activity and diet which can also support a healthy lifestyle. The PSHE Association (2015) rightly suggests that PSHE should not be delivered in isolation.

The PSHE Association has published an extremely useful programme of study guidance (PSHE Association, 2015) which shows how PSHE, mental health and emotional well-being may be integrated into the curriculum. This could mean from Key Stage 1 to Key Stage 4 for example, linking teaching to the overarching themes of:

- health and well-being;

- relationships;

- living in the wider world.

(PSHE Association, 2015, p5)

If you require further support regarding the understanding, planning and implementation of the PSHE Association's programme guidance in your setting, this may be found at **www.pshe-association. org.uk/sites/default/files/Mental%20health%20guidance.pdf**.

PSHE should be embedded into the educational life of an individual learner through a spiral of learning that will revisit as well as promote positive behaviours by challenging and meeting the needs of children and young people as they grow older. This may be achieved through whole school strategies such as circle time and SEAL, Brain Gym, visiting speakers' reflection time, and work around anti-bullying. For some of the most vulnerable in our care consideration must also be given over how best to prevent shared experiences becoming too personal throughout PSHE. Strategies to support such individuals may be found by the use of role play and puppets to provide advice in non-real situations, which may allow for the exploration of dealing with such scenarios (PSHE Association, 2015). As Weare (2015) and the PSHE Association (2015) indicate, for learning to be effective it needs to provide good problem-solving skills. PSHE can

> promote the skills, knowledge, understanding and language that will enable pupils to adopt healthy thoughts, behaviours and strategies and to seek appropriate and timely support when they or a friend need it.

(PSHE Association, 2015)

Through empowering learners to make decisions about their lives in a safe and supportive environment, each individual can use their experiences to make informed decisions about how best in practice to deal with the situation and issues that are eroding their mental and emotional well-being.

Such empowerment may be seen as that of a 'growth mind-set' which allows individuals to feel in control of their own abilities and skills in order to facilitate change (PSHE Association, 2015). PSHE may also promote positive relationships between professionals and those in their charge so that each individual feels valued and so that strategies can be deployed to best support the most vulnerable of children and young people.

Though PSHE should pervade the curriculum, despite the best of planning it is important to realise that at times PSHE may also need to respond to situations that are immediate and current for both individuals and for their settings. For example, an issue such as the severe injury or death of a pupil, which can affect children and young people's mental health and well-being, may require discrete teaching.

Additional guidance to support the teaching of PSHE in your setting may be found at **www. pshe-association.org.uk**. Similarly should you need any guidance, help or advice on supporting the prevention of drug and alcohol related issues in your setting, further information may be found at **http://mentor-adepis.org**.

 **KEY REFLECTIONS**

- How might the SMSC and PSHE curriculum underpin the teaching and learning related to mental health and well-being?
- How might other aspects of the curriculum support such an agenda?

The voice of children and young people

As Weare (2015) indicates, since mental health and well-being rests on an individual's ability to have a sense of control and self-efficacy it is important that children and young people feel they have a genuine voice, that they are consulted about decisions regarding their own learning and that of school life, and that their rights are respected and listened to. Not only is this vital, but under Article 12 of the United Nations Convention on the Rights of the Child:

> *Children have the right to express their views freely and for their views to be given due weight in matters affecting them.*

> (Robinson, 2014, p18)

Healthy Schools (2007) point out that children and young people's involvement should not be tokenistic, but for it to be empowering it should be realistic and meaningful. Robinson (2014) suggests that in schools that take a rights respecting approach there may a reduction in incidents of bullying as well as an improved ability for individuals to deal with conflicts they encounter. However, such an approach involves the need to avoid the temptation of listening to the most vocal and motivated of children and young people (Healthy Schools, 2007; Weare, 2015). It is important for settings to realise that it is often those who are most marginalised who are struggling to be heard and are in need of listening to the most. Therefore, schools must do all that they can to promote inclusion amongst all individuals and to promote their involvement in change, that comes from them and is not part of a predetermined agenda. If children and young people are to feel connected to their setting and to make a meaningful contribution to the decisions that affect their school lives and future well-being then there must be an equal and honest dialogue between individuals and adults. Therefore mechanisms such as school councils should represent the range of individuals in a setting and hence of the opinion expressed. Not only does such a body need to be inclusive, but it must be given status and the children and young people should be taught and given the skills necessary to promote the democratic system they are involved in. As Weare (2015) suggests, pupil voice when effective promotes a defensive, school connection which can lead to an enhanced feeling towards self, as well as promoting social skills. Individuals in a school that has a rights respecting approach feel valued, respected, cared for and listened to (Robinson, 2014). All of this should be embedded in relationships with staff where genuine concern is shown toward well-being.

Other school based strategies that a setting might provide to promote dialogue and involvement include:

- pupil interviews or pupil based evaluations of school based activities;

- questions on parent questionnaires;

- assessment for learning approaches such as smiley/sad faces, thumbs up;

- presenting at assemblies;

- reporting back on actions and decisions made by School or Eco-Councils;

- suggestion/worry boxes;

- opportunities through PSHE/SEAL/circle time activities to share;

- opportunities outside of lesson time for adults to share conversation such as out of school activities;

- relationships in nurture groups or with assigned/named adults.

In some settings, pupils' voices can be harnessed in what may be called peer mentoring/peer review or peer support in order to support and improve pupils' well-being. This approach can prove effective if children and young people are given suitable and appropriate support and training. Given such induction they may then be able to proactively work in schools in some form of buddying or peer support approach. This may lead to the promotion of social and emotional skills amongst their peers or the ability to model alternative ways of thinking and behaving (Weare, 2015). DfE (2016) suggests in some settings this can offer an effective, as well as low cost, support to individuals which can act as a preventative measure against low levels of self-esteem. Weare (2015), however, indicates that the success of such schemes may be found in terms of the ownership and engagement it provides for children or young people.

For children with behaviour, emotional and social difficulties (BESD) a useful approach is 'circle of friends' (Farrell, 2006 cited in Cole, 2015). This allows an individual to explore the feelings and issues being created between individuals involved in the scenario during each other's absence. By promoting a sense of empathy with the situation and individuals involved, an agreement can be forged between each party about the best way forward to improve the situation encountered for the better.

Outside the school setting, organisations such as MIND provide comprehensive peer support for a range of issues, and further information may be found by accessing their website: **www.mind.org. uk/get-involved/peer-support**.

KEY REFLECTIONS

- Why are children and young people's voices so important in promoting their positive mental health and well-being?
- How might a school facilitate and promote the establishment of the voice of an individual?
- How might peers be used to support an inclusive school environment?

Staff and continuing professional development

Teachers who do not have any specialist mental health and well-being training can be left to feel ill-equipped and lacking in confidence to identify and deal with the huge range of mental health and well-being issues being presented by children and young people in their everyday teaching lives. As Public Health England (2015) indicates, if school staff are to be equipped to identify mental health issues in their learning population, then they need access to continuing professional development (CPD) training so as to increase their knowledge of this important aspect of school life. Cole (2015) notes that school staff also need training not only to understand the importance that pastoral support can provide but also with regard to accessing specialist support services such as child and adolescent mental health services (CAMHS).

Ongoing CPD is also necessary for teachers to receive training in order to support the ever-evolving issues which can lead to issues for the mental health and emotional well-being of individuals. For example:

- The Child Exploitation and Online Protection Command, or CEOP, offers training to reduce issues around cyberbullying and CSE (child sexual exploitation).
- Prevent (part of the government's counter-terrorism strategy) – training linked to the safeguarding of children around issues of radicalisation.
- Child protection/safeguarding training.

Therefore, it is important that the leadership and management of any setting promotes regular CPD for its teachers as a central part in promoting a whole school approach to supporting mental health and well-being, not only for its staff, but also the children and young people in its care. Not only should this form part of any whole school aspiration, but given Ofsted's (2015) view on CPD that it can have a positive impact on teachers' teaching as well as pupils' learning, it should form a vital part of all schools' improvement planning to make them an outstanding institution.

However, despite the best laid plans to support staff development, barriers may exist to stop the effective delivery of teachers' professional development. First, given the limited funding of some school budgets, planned CPD course budgets may have to be used to focus on school improvement agenda, perhaps linked to a recent Ofsted inspection or to supporting the effective delivery of core subjects such as literacy and numeracy. Research by the Education Policy Institute has shown how the long hours worked by English teachers, compared to those of most other countries, have hindered their access to continuing professional development (Frith, 2016). Given the many challenges faced with workforce development linked to children's and young people's mental health, it is important to *be clear about who you need in your team and if they have the right skills to the roles you need them for* (Frith, 2016, p36).

Mental health and well-being CPD may take many forms in schools but it should be founded on a clear assessment of a teacher's professional needs as well as on what is needed to support whole school development. This may be achieved through the use of a school's performance management systems so as to encourage, challenge and support teachers' improvement (Ofsted, 2015). However, although CPD may be seen as being a particular course of training to support an individual's needs, at times for the promotion of consistency of an approach in a setting, whole school training may be needed. This may be achieved through using items such as teacher development days for the most effective means of delivering CPD.

Not all staff development should be seen to centre on teachers being allowed to go out of school in order to be trained to promote the personal and social development of its pupils. MindEd is a free educational resource on children and young people's mental health, which offers e-learning modules that any adult with an interest in this area can access. There are options to dip in and out around subject areas or to complete whole modules and gain certificates of learning. MindEd also provides children and young people's mental health e-learning aimed at families; if parents express concern or an interest in their child's mental health and well-being, it may be useful to direct them to this resource, which can be accessed at **www.minded.org.uk**. Ofsted (2006) suggests that for some less experienced and newly appointed staff, assigning them an experienced school mentor can also be seen as being beneficial to supporting the needs of their many pupils. This may involve the adoption of a coaching and team teaching approach for staff as a means of building the capacity of less experienced teachers when dealing with pupils with BESD.

If you require further information to support your training of CEOP, Prevent or child sexual exploitation please visit **www.ceop.police.uk** and **www.preventforschools.org** or **http://paceuk.info/about-cse/keep-them-safe**.

KEY REFLECTIONS

- Why is professional CPD so important?
- What might prove a barrier to providing CPD?
- How might in-school CPD be supported?

Partnership with parents, carers and outside agencies

When supporting any child or young person with regard to mental health and well-being, it is vital that a partnership is forged between parents, carers and families to secure the best outcomes. As Weare (2015) acknowledges, the effectiveness in this partnership lies in the support and understanding of a child/young person's needs that parents and carers can offer schools. This may be in addition to the role schools can play in developing and supporting their parenting skills and attitudes towards any such issues. By supporting parents and carers through what often are challenging scenarios for their most vulnerable of charges a school can help improve relationships, through mutual co-operation as well as making them more ready to engage with learning and the school setting. As the DfE (2016) indicates, such collaborative partnerships between parents and carers can lead to an improved likelihood of reducing a child/young person's difficulties as well as the ability to support their emotional development (given the child/young person's appropriate consent). When considering the issue of partnerships, not only is such a collaboration desirable but it is an expectation of Ofsted (2015) that schools engage with parents and carers in order to support their child/young person's safety, spiritual, moral, social and cultural development alongside guidance to help support their improvement. The school setting may be able to signpost some more vulnerable parents to agencies such as Parent Partnership in order to allow them to be given the appropriate guidance and support in order to better help their child.

Given that children may be in care in our school communities, it is also important that settings have clear strategies to promote successful partnership with foster carers, members of the extended families and social workers. For looked after children such clear mechanisms can provide a vital bridge to support what is happening in the home setting and how this may be mitigated against when in the school setting.

Allied to this partnership it is important that settings engage with outside agencies to support a child/young person's mental health and well-being. Such provision in some cases is arranged and/or funded by the setting directly themselves depending on their funding arrangements, for example loss or bereavement counselling. Outside agencies, through their specialised knowledge of how best to identify needs and of the range of support available to individuals, are often best placed to provide support outside that of the school's expertise and graduated response. External partnerships are seen by Ofsted (2015) as a means of allowing leaders to identify and support children and young people effectively. Such support may take the form of in-school input with specialist support by professionals such as the school nurse/health visitor, educational psychologists or through outside interventions by their general practitioner (GP), CAMHS practitioners or paediatric consultants. However, whatever support is provided there will need to be a close collaboration between such agencies and the school so that appropriate and complementary support may be given to the child or young person when in their educational setting. In some cases it may be that not only will the school have to use outside agencies to support children and young people but such support may also be needed to support family members as a whole through their own mental health and emotional problems. Taking such actions may prove the best route in order to best support the individual at the centre of a school's concerns. As children and young people also get older it will be a school's duty to signpost to agencies that can discuss and support them with personal and emotional issues. To find out more information regarding the range of support and services available to you to support the mental health and well-being of your children and young people, visit the Youth Wellbeing Directory at **www.youthwellbeing.co.uk**.

KEY REFLECTIONS

- Why are partnerships with parents and carers vital?
- How might a school use outside agencies to support their mental health and well-being agenda?
- Why is it so important for schools to have a whole school approach to mental health and well-being?
- What strategic role can leadership and management play in such an approach?
- What role can the school ethos, culture and environment play in supporting individual mental health and well-being?
- How can the school curriculum and school practice complement and support the work of the school?
- How can the voice of children and young people support and enhance the whole school approach?
- Why is CPD necessary to support professionals, children and young people?
- How can working with parents, carers and outside agency support a school's approach to mental health and well-being?

CHAPTER SUMMARY

- Mental health and well-being is most effectively dealt with through a whole school approach.
- The school's leadership and management can play a pivotal role in providing a vision and means to support the mental health and well-being needs of its stakeholders.
- Providing the right ethos, culture and environment can best support individuals both in the school and classroom.
- The curriculum and practice of a school can significantly contribute to a climate in which children and young adults with mental health and well-being issues can flourish.
- The voice of individuals can serve to inform and enhance an understanding of how best to support children and young people in their setting.
- The continuing professional development of school staff will help them all have a clear role to play in identifying and supporting children with behavioural issues linked to their mental health and well-being.
- The partnerships between parents, carers and outside agencies are fundamental in facilitating a holistic approach to providing support for children and young adults.

━━ FURTHER READING ━━

Boingboing provides opportunities to learn more about promoting resilience: www.boingboing.org.uk.

MIND (2016) *Making sense of peer support*. Available at: http://mind.org.uk/information-support/drugs-and-treatments/peer-support/peer-support-for-specific-groups/#.WByT5IXXIdU (accessed 4 November 2016).

Young Minds (2016) *About self-esteem*. Available at: www.youngminds.org.uk/for_parents/whats_worrying_you_about_your_child/self-esteem/about_self-esteem (accessed 1 January 2016).

━━ REFERENCES ━━

Banerjee, R., McLaughlin, C., Cotney, J., Roberts, L. and Peereboom, C. (2016) *Promoting emotional health, well-being and resilience in primary schools*. Available at: http://ppiw.org.uk/files/2016/02/PPIW-Report-Promoting-Emotional-Health-Well-being-and-Resilience-in-Primary-Schools-Final.pdf (accessed 25 September 2016).

Brooks, F. (2012) *Life stages: School years*, in Annual Report of the Chief Medical Officer (2012) *Our children deserve better: Prevention pays*. Available at: www.gov.uk/government/uploads/system/uploads/attachment_data/file/252657/33571_2901304_CMO_Chapter_7.pdf (accessed 23 July 2016).

Cole, T. (2015) *Mental health difficulties and children at risk of exclusion from schools in England: A review from an educational perspective of policy, practice and research, 1997 to 2015*. Available at: www.education.ox.ac.uk/wordpress/wp-content/uploads/2015/02/MENTAL-HEALTH-AND-EXCLUSION-FINAL-DIGITAL-13-06-15.pdf (accessed 23 September 2016).

Cowie, H., Boardman, C., Dawkins, J. and Dawn, J. (2004) *Emotional Health and Wellbeing: A Practical Guide for Schools*. London: Paul Chapman Publishing.

Department for Education (DfE) (2013) *Personal, social, health and economic (PSHE) education*. Available at: www.gov.uk/government/publications/personal-social-health-and-economic-education-pshe/personal-social-health-and-economic-pshe-education (accessed 13 November 2016).

Department for Education (2014) *National curriculum in England*. Available at: www.gov.uk/government/collections/national-curriculum (accessed 12 November 2016).

Department for Education (2016) *Mental health and behaviour in schools*. Available at: www.gov.uk/government/publications/mental-health-and-behaviour-in-schools—2 (accessed 12 September 2016).

Department of Health (DoH) (2015) *Future in mind: Promoting, protecting and improving our children and young people's mental health and wellbeing*. Available at: www.gov.uk/government/uploads/system/uploads/attachment_data/file/414024/Childrens_Mental_Health.pdf (accessed 16 October 2016).

Farrell, M. (2006) *Behavioural, Emotional and Social Difficulties: Practical Strategies*. London: David Fulton Publishers.

Frith, E. (2016) *Children's and Young People's Mental Health: Time to Deliver*. London: Education Policy Unit.

Healthy Schools (2007) *Guidance for schools on developing emotional health and wellbeing*. Available at: www.healthyschools.london.gov.uk/sites/default/files/EHWB.pdf (accessed 4 November 2016).

NCB/ASCL (2016) *Keeping young people in mind: Findings from a survey of schools across England*. Available at: www.ncb.org.uk/sites/default/files/field/attachment/news/ascl_and_ncb_findings_from_survey_briefing_final_footnotes.pdf (accessed 13 February 2017).

Newson, R. (2016) *School leaders voice concerns over children's mental health care*. Available at: www.ncb.org.uk/news-opinion/news-highlights/school-leaders-voice-concerns-over-childrens-mental-health-care (accessed 12 November 2016).

Ofsted (2005) *Managing challenging behaviours*. Available at: www2.yorksj.ac.uk/pdf/managing_challenging_behaviour2.pdf (accessed 12 October 2016).

Ofsted (2006) *Inclusion: Does it matter where pupils are taught? Provision and outcomes in different settings for pupils with learning difficulties and disabilities*. Available at: http://dera.ioe.ac.uk/6001/1/Inclusion%20does%20it%20matter%20where%20pupils%20are%20taught%20(pdf%20format)%20.pdf (accessed 17 November 2016).

Ofsted (2015) *School inspection handbook*. Available at: www.gov.uk/government/publications/school-inspection-handbook-from-september-2015 (accessed 12 November 2016).

PSHE Association (2015) *Teacher guidance: Preparing to teach about mental health and emotional wellbeing*. Available at: www.pshe-association.org.uk/sites/default/files/Mental%20health%20guidance.pdf (accessed 10 November 2016).

Public Health England (2014) *The link between pupil health and wellbeing and attainment*. Available at: www.gov.uk/government/uploads/system/uploads/attachment_data/file/370686/HT_briefing_layout vFINALvii.pdf (accessed 18 September 2016).

Public Health England (2015) *Promoting children and young people's emotional health and wellbeing: A whole school and college approach*. Available at: www.gov.uk/government/uploads/system/uploads/attachment_data/file/414908/Final_EHWB_draft_20_03_15.pdf (accessed 5 October 2016).

Robinson, C. (2014) *Children, Their Voices and Their Experiences of School: What Does That Tell Us?* Cambridge Primary Review Trust: University of York.

Stirling, S. and Emery, H. (2016) *A whole school framework for emotional well-being and mental health*. Available at: www.ncb.org.uk/sites/default/files/field/attachment/NCB%20School%20Well%20Being%20Framework%20Leaders%20Tool%20FINAL.pdf (accessed 9 August 2016).

Weare, K. (2015) *What Works in Promoting Social and Emotional Well-being and Responding to Mental Health Problems in School?* London: National Children's Bureau.

Weare, K. and Nind, M. (2011) Mental health promotion and problem prevention in schools: What does the evidence say? *Health Promotion International*, 26: 29–69. Available at: http://heapro.oxfordjournals.org/content/26/suppl_1/i29.full (accessed 21 November 2016).

Wyn, J., Cahill, H., Holdworth, R., Rowling, L. and Carson, S. (2000) Mindmatters: A whole school approach promoting mental health and wellbeing. Available at: www.researchgate.net/publications 12367371 (accessed 14 August 2016).

3

CHILDREN AND YOUNG PEOPLE'S BEHAVIOUR: WHAT IS BEING COMMUNICATED AND HOW SHOULD WE RESPOND?

Chapter objectives

By the end of this chapter you should be aware of:

- the current issues relating to supporting positive behaviours in children and young people in an educational setting;
- the role professionals may play in understanding, promoting and supporting positive behaviour;
- the range of strategies and policy guidelines that can support children and young people who present with challenging behaviours in school;
- the barriers to supporting children and young people with behavioural difficulties;
- why it is important to always consider behaviour in a context of curiosity about what is being communicated;
- why unacceptable behaviours become a medium for acting out from a stress position.

Teachers' Standards

This chapter supports the development of the following Teachers' Standards:

TS1: Set high expectations which inspire, motivate and challenge pupils

- Demonstrate consistently the positive attitudes, values and behaviour which are expected of pupils.

TS7: Manage behaviour effectively to ensure a good and safe learning environment

- Have clear rules and routines for behaviour in classrooms, and take responsibility for promoting good and courteous behaviour both in classrooms and around the school, in accordance with the school's behaviour policy.
- Have high expectations of behaviour, and establish a framework for discipline with a range of strategies, using praise, sanctions and rewards consistently and fairly.
- Manage classes effectively, using approaches which are appropriate to pupils' needs in order to involve and motivate them.
- Maintain good relationships with pupils, exercise appropriate authority, and act decisively when necessary.

Introduction

This chapter will focus on understanding the behaviour of children and young people in the class and wider school setting. Consideration will be given to potential links with mental health and well-being. It will also examine the risk factors that may generate negative behaviours and the challenges that practitioners may face. The impact of these behaviours on the child/young person themselves, their families and the individual's educational setting will also be explored. Finally, it will offer strategies to support children and young people within the educational setting so that they may successfully enjoy and participate appropriately in school life.

Why be concerned?

As children and young people develop and mature, managing changing emotions as a result of the maturation process can prove to be an understandable and unpredictable challenge. Physiological changes driven by hormonal activity alongside the child or young person's own personality and character can lead to issues around a range of positive and negative behaviours to be observed in any educational setting for many children and young people. For some children, allied to these normal maturation stages of development, are the additional issues centred on risk factors such as environmental and contextual considerations; for example, violence and poverty, the family, domestic abuse and child abuse. This may all in turn lead to the young person/child themselves developing attachment difficulties, neurodevelopmental difficulties and conditions (such as attention deficit hyperactivity disorder, or ADHD), and low self-esteem (Young Minds, 2016). All of these examples can lead to heightened levels of anxiety which is very difficult for children and young people to manage in a manner acceptable to the school environment. Sadly, it would not be uncommon for some children and young people to have experience of, and be subject to, many of these areas of difficulty. Government statistics (DfE, 2016b) suggest that risk factors such as social disadvantage, family adversity and cognitive or attention problems have a cumulative impact upon children developing behaviour problems. Boys under the age of 10 who have five or more risk factors are almost 11 times more likely to exhibit conduct disorder compared to those with no risk factors. Girls similarly were also 19 times more likely to exhibit conduct disorder given five or more risk factors compared again to those with no risk factors. Statistics indicate that a minimum of three children per classroom have a potential mental health problem and that these can often be present through difficult and challenging behaviours; all teaching and school staff will therefore have an experience of this. It is through extrapolations by researchers such as Cole (2015) that we can start to appreciate the impact and scale of the issues faced by our schools with regard to managing children and young people who experience social, emotional and behavioural difficulties (SEBD).

It is really important to remember to try and re-frame behaviour in a psychological sense and try and understand what is being communicated. A child acting out in class, perhaps being the 'class clown', will distract the teacher and will often have a response that may be 'telling off' but the behaviour becomes re-enforced as other pupils may find the child popular. If we consider the child may not be able to manage or understand the classroom activity or task that has been set, then automatically anxiety levels become raised. As we discussed earlier, biologically, there has to be a response in order to be able to manage the anxiety at a level which can be tolerated. So being a 'clown' immediately relieves one from the anxiety-provoking task. Being 'told off' does not escalate anxiety to such a high level so relief is experienced and thus the behaviour unwittingly becomes re-enforced. It is estimated that 400,000–500,000 children will be faced with the risk of exclusion related to SEBD issues. Exclusion, despite it always being a last resort, is probably one of the most detrimental interventions for individual children and young people, further reinforcing a low sense of worth and removing contact with potentially the only professionals and a 'safe' setting in the young person's life. It should also be noted that punishment does not work for the majority of children who present with challenging behaviours; withholding play and break time activity is often counter-productive and therefore should be avoided.

Children who have attachment difficulties are likely to present with behaviour problems in the classroom. It is important to remember that attachment is the main mechanism for the regulation of relationships (Schore, 2005). The quality of attachment is determined by early experiences and these predict lifelong relationship patterns. Secondary attachment figures such as school staff can provide reliable sources of safety and comfort. In early years settings there are requirements for consistent key workers. Remember the principle of attachment is about internalising a sense of self and safety. The emotional activity within relationships becomes the supportive factor and children and young people develop hierarchies of attachment figures which would include school staff significant to them. Children and young people with an insecure attachment quality experience raised cortisol levels (the stress response hormone) even in fairly mild scary situations. Heightened anxiety initiates a stress response understood as fight, flight or freeze. Typically, a young person may take the fight response and become very challenging and confrontational in the classroom. The experience of 'rejection' following such an outburst, rather than a contained response, is likely to further escalate the attachment behaviour. Whilst this may not mitigate the behaviour or mean there should not be a proportionate response, it is necessary and helpful to understand the 'back story' and context.

Children and young people with a diagnosis of ADHD commonly have difficulties with the 'triad of impairments' which include:

- hyperactivity;

- difficulties with concentration;

- impulsivity.

It is easy, therefore, to appreciate how tricky the average classroom environment is to negotiate with this diagnosis. Yet, there is an expectation these children and young people will somehow manage. Many do but it can be helpful to include strategies such as time out cards and additional 1:1 support to help with classroom tasks. It can help to positively reframe ADHD as a child or young person with bags of energy and get up and go spirit. The traditional classroom can be a difficult and challenging place for many children. They often do remarkably well in alternative education settings that include more of an outside land-based curriculum.

The challenge for schools with regard to managing children and young people's behaviour would therefore seem more than evident given such figures. Researchers such as Weare (2015) indicate that 1 in 4 children and young people have a clinically identified mental health disorder and/or emotional behaviour problem that can limit their development and learning, whilst over 5 per cent of children, in particular boys, exhibit anti-social, behaviour and conduct disorder conditions. Furthermore, a survey by the Association of Teachers and Lecturers (ATL) reported that

> *the number of pupils in the UK with behavioural and mental health problems is on the rise.*

> (Sellgren, 2013, p1)

It is important that appropriate provision is given to successfully support such pupils and young people and any of their associated challenging behaviours to reach their full educational potential. Given the expectations that schools are placed under with regard to securing suitable levels of behaviour (Steer, 2011; DfE, 2016a) appropriate support and provision would seem to be of paramount importance if such individuals are to have a bright education in our school systems.

Whole school behaviour policy

Though there may be many triggers for a range of behaviours, which may include unacceptable mental or physical acts towards another child or adult, schools have a duty to manage such issues consistently using their mandatory whole school behaviour policy (DfE, 2012). The behaviour policy, though site-specific, may be underpinned by additional government advice such as 'Mental health and behaviour in schools' (DfE, 2016b) which may serve to help schools understand how they can support children with disruptive behaviour. Children and young people who are depressed, anxious or withdrawn do not usually present with challenging behaviours in class; on the contrary their behaviour is often quiet and withdrawn and is less likely to attract concern, but nevertheless there should be equal concern and an appropriate response for these children.

Having a whole school behaviour policy will provide individuals with a template for behaviour and the provision for the promotion of a positive learning environment so that all staff and pupils can feel safe and that they belong. Any such policy, under its duty of care to promote equality and diversity, should promote fairness, equality and respect for every pupil no matter what the triggers may be for their behaviours. This policy will normally outline the different strategies to ensure that a pupil's treatment is equitable and consistent. However, it is important to note that despite such generic school policy guidance, as educators we will all react and operate differently when encountering what may often be seen as context-specific disruptive behaviours linked to an individual's emotional and social difficulties. For educators to be successful in such contexts, they should be

> *well organised, consistent, humorous, calm, enthusiastic, skilful in delivering their specialist subjects, set clear boundaries, flexible, understand 'behaviour' causation and empathetic.*

> (Cole, 2015, p42)

More generic strategies that might be outlined in the policy to support positive behaviour may include, for example:

- individually and group agreed class or school and class rules;

- peer mentoring and buddying arrangements;

- a framework for rewards and sanctions;

- PSHE class-based intervention such as circle time;

- specific targeted interventions strategies such as the use of socially speaking and nurture groups;

- additional staffing.

However, for any behaviour policy to be successful in promoting class-based practice which best manages challenging behaviour, it is important that it is underpinned by professionals who know their children and young people well. That there are educators who will spend time to get to the root of any unacceptable behaviours rather than just reacting to what can understandably be a disruption to teaching and others being educated. For any education to be successful it should nurture a positive classroom ethos which is founded on good relationships, and where respect is underpinned by a genuine interest in the child or young person who is exhibiting the challenging behaviour (Ofsted, 2005).

Though only medical professionals can make a formal clinical diagnosis of a mental health difficulty that can influence a child's behaviour, schools are well placed to observe changes in a child's behaviour due to their daily contact with their children or young adults. Such observations may well provide clues and insight into the root causes of issues. Relationships will also provide the key to understanding a child's behaviour. For some of our most vulnerable of children, educational professionals may be the only adult they may learn to trust and feel that they are understood by and have consistent contact with. Often knowledge of a child will be built up over time as will the strategies that support behaviour; however, in some situations mental health and behaviour may deteriorate quickly, perhaps triggered by an adverse external experience or factor. When noticing any changes in an individual's behaviour it is worth considering the following:

- Is there behaviour out of character compared to their normal actions and responses?

- Has the child appeared worried or starting talking to you about issues that are concerning them?

- Is there a particular time of day, group of individuals or relationship that triggers an adverse behaviour?

- Has the change in the behaviour been sudden or gradual?

- What has the responsible adult told you about the child recently and may that be causing a trigger for the behaviour, for example, a life change such as moving house, loss or separation such as birth of a sibling or a traumatic incident such as an accident?

KEY REFLECTIONS

- What factors may lead to issues around an individual's behaviour?
- How might a whole school behaviour policy lead to the support of behavioural inclusion?
- How might professional relationships support the behavioural inclusion of an individual?

CASE STUDY: PAULINE

Over the last couple of months Pauline, aged 10, has often come to school about 10 minutes after the school day has started. She is reluctant to come into the classroom and will often stand outside the door waiting to come in. When the teacher approaches Pauline she will be seen by other pupils backing away from the door and not wanting to engage with the teacher who is trying her best to coax Pauline into class. Pauline does, however, tell her class teacher that she does not want to be laughed at by the pupils when she comes in.

Case study reflections

- How long has this been happening for and is it an ongoing issue or something that may have happened to Pauline recently which might explain such a behavioural change?
- What does the class teacher need to do to start to understand Pauline's ongoing lateness?
- Why is Pauline reluctant to come into class?
- How might this lateness be affecting Pauline's mental health and well-being?

Though the teacher knows that Pauline is a sensitive child, the lateness issue has been brought on by her mother having to look after her elderly mother. The class teacher has not been told by the mother that she is finding routines difficult and that due to tiredness she is not waking up early enough in the morning to do all the things needed to get Pauline to school, which is making her late. Pauline's lateness is making her embarrassed and she does not like the other children laughing at her which is affecting her self-esteem and peer friendships. Pauline is also conscious that when she is late she has missed the start of the lesson which makes it hard for her to understand what is going on. The class teacher needs to be talking to both Pauline and her mother to see how the school can support her together with the school SENCo to see if she can access support through the school nurse or her doctor if necessary. Pauline's mother should also be advised to contact adult social care services to gain support with caring for her elderly mother. In the short term, the class teacher needs to find a strategy to help Pauline to come into class without her friends just thinking she is late again. Perhaps an arrangement may be made with another teacher or classroom assistant that Pauline appears to be late into class since she has been delayed by them on an errand and that she brings an item into class with the excuse collecting the item has made her late.

Barriers to relationships

As the Department for Education (2016b, p24) suggests:

> *if parents/carers can be supported to better manage their children's behaviour, alongside work being carried out with the child at school, there is a much greater likelihood of success in reducing the child's problems, and in supporting their academic and emotional development.*

It is important that, where possible, parents and carers work alongside the school to provide a cornerstone for you as an educational professional to support children and young people in your setting. Schools can offer not only someone who will listen but also they can provide sign-posting to agencies that can, for example, support them individually or as a family. The value of this partnership has been recognised in reports such as Ofsted (2009), where strong relationships are seen as being fundamental to success. Parents and the extended family should be welcomed into school, and valued, and clear expectations set such as the value of a co-operative 'whole school' approach that embraces the child and young person, the school, families and the community.

However, in some situations, barriers will arise and you may find that parents or carers are very reluctant for you to get to know them and understand the root cause of behaviour in a child; they may also not take kindly to advice or signposting to parenting groups. This in itself may form further barriers to supporting the child or young person or to finding effective strategies or identifying other agencies who may support you with this issue. Individuals may be reluctant to engage with you for a range of reasons:

- a personal fear of engaging with an educational setting due to their own negative experiences;

- personal embarrassment or loss of pride due to an issue;

- child protection issues being identified;

- fear of intervention of other support services linked to their own personal experience or perceived impact upon the family.

Given a reluctance to engage, it may be hard to gain their confidence and consent. Such situations, however, can be overcome with time and patience. Strategies that may support and enable parents'/carers' engagement might include:

- letting parents know when their children have been successful, not just when there was a problem;

- the school's open door policy;

- establishing firm links before the children started school, often visiting parents at home;

- the involvement of a school's learning mentor or a Parent Support Advisor who might be able to open up a dialogue given their lack of direct class-based link with the child;

- an induction meeting to review how the individual is settling into their new setting;

- targeting of pupil premium funding if there is a link to social disadvantage to support fun, non-academic activities with both the child and parent/carer that may promote a positive relationship with the setting;

- signposting to outside agencies and resources such as MindEd, Relate or Women's Aid.

For some settings where there is a constant turnover of pupils on roll, getting to know an individual may prove challenging when managing behaviour which may be linked to mental health and well-being. This will often make it hard to initially assess what the issues are and to respond appropriately to the pupils' needs. If you receive a child or young person such as this, their school records from their previous setting will prove an excellent base to start your understanding of what are the triggers for the child's behaviour and what strategies are most effective and appropriate. If you find that the records do not really help you understand your new child, your next port of call could be to contact their last setting to talk to the head teacher or their prior class teacher about the child. This should be done in consultation with the head teacher and SENCo. Such a conversation will sometimes provide more detailed background knowledge on this child or young person's history, the issues they have faced and the most successful strategies to support them.

However, whatever the barriers and the trigger for behaviours relating to a child's mental health and well-being, for any approach to be successful it must be supported by an agreed whole school ethos which involves the head teachers, senior leaders and governors, creating a culture where the duty of care for safeguarding individuals is seen as of paramount importance. Such an approach is clearly supported by research which suggests that low exclusion rates may be achieved in schools that promote an inclusive whole school community approach both in their policy and practice when dealing with issues linked to individuals' mental health (Cole, 2015). As Cole (2015, p41) notes with regard to the establishment of an inclusive school climate:

> it requires a 'critical mass' of staff committed to inclusive values, who seek to avoid the exclusion of children, seeing this as failure on the part of their school. Their beliefs and practice influence colleagues around them ... Teamwork is the norm and a collegiate approach, frequently talking and listening to each other – as well as hearing the voices of young people.

In promoting an inclusive environment, it would be hoped that such a shared responsibility for the support of such individuals will be underpinned in an ethos where individuals can talk openly and honestly about the problems they encounter when dealing with the most challenging of behaviours. As Weare (2015) suggests, staying open-minded, calm and reflective helps the educational professional to allow for positive choices to be identified, to move the situation forward, and allows them to provide a positive role model for the child and young adult as well as helping them to manage their own emotional stress. Allied to this, it is also vital that professionals are allowed to engage in appropriate continued professional development if they are to best support our most vulnerable of children and young adults.

KEY REFLECTIONS

- What might be some of the key barriers that may stop parents and carers engaging with support for children and young people with behavioural issues?
- What strategies may be implemented to overcome these barriers to support?
- How might a setting maximise their knowledge of children and young people who join their setting with behavioural issues?

CASE STUDY: TYLER

Tyler has just started the new school year in Year 2. He has just celebrated his fifth birthday and is the tallest child in the class of 25 children. There is a teacher and teaching assistant, Mrs Brown and Miss Smith.

Tyler is often in trouble in class, usually for not staying on task and for getting up and walking around, looking at and often interrupting the other children, especially when the work involves writing practice and number work. Outside the classroom in the playground Tyler loves running around and playing tag, and he appears built for speed compared to some of his peers.

He can quickly get into arguments with the other children if they don't go along with his wishes around playing in a particular way. He gets angry very quickly if things are not going his way and will hit or kick the child he is having a disagreement with. Most of the other children (usually the other boys) will back off when challenged and some refuse to play or join in with him. Most of the children have known Tyler since pre-school so are used to his angry displays which erupt quickly and subside equally quickly.

Case study reflections

- For Tyler, this is not a new or a change in behaviour; he has always tended to behave in this way.
- What works in terms of managing his behaviour? How did his pre-school teachers deal with this?
- Could this be connected to ADHD perhaps? He does not sit still for long and struggles to concentrate in class-related tasks that involve writing or numbers.
- How does he get on in PE or other sports or outdoor activities?

Tyler is the tallest of his peers and appears as an older child of 7 so there often seems to be a general higher expectation of him around behaviour especially, but he is only just 5. He probably uses this to his advantage – it can be experienced by the others as intimidating, as he has quite a strong temperament and presence. So, he is both physically strong in appearance, but also psychologically in character, though he will not have the associated emotional maturity or strength.

Teaching staff are working closely with Mum and have a good relationship with her as Tyler can also be quite a challenge at home. At home Mum is often tired and Tyler is used to getting his own way and for things to be on his terms.

It is important for both school and Mum to work together to aim for a consistent approach as this will be the most effective. Mum may need additional support with this which could also include Granddad, who is close to Tyler.

Tyler and Mum are very close, which can lead to Tyler being quite omnipotent towards her so it is easy to see how this learnt behaviour becomes transferred to other situations, such as at school and with peers. Tyler had a poor start in life in terms of relationships. Dad left during the pregnancy and Tyler has no contact with him. Mum has since had other relationships but is on her own again now. Tyler's father and one of his step-fathers had problems around emotional regulation and anger and were abusive towards Mum and Tyler. The maternal granddad helps out with looking after Tyler and does the school run when Mum is at work.

Tyler has experienced relationships that are unpredictable in terms of their behaviour and what will happen next, and people who leave and abandon him, which has led to anxiety in all of his future relationships. He may also feel it is his responsibility to 'protect' Mum – perhaps he has done so in the past? To do so requires a level of control-taking and omnipotence but it is not appropriate to continue in this way and can lead to trouble, as we have seen.

Children like Tyler are often misunderstood and in the desire to seek answers or provide a 'label' professionals may seek a medical explanation such as ADHD or attachment disorder, which is not a picture here. It is a combination of a child with a quick temperament (perhaps like his father), who appears older than his chronological age so there are greater expectations of him socially and cognitively, but who also actually appears as quite a presence. He has a good relationship with Mum and Granddad and despite his 'flare ups' remains popular. It is much easier to understand Tyler with the knowledge of his and his family experiences.

Given his athleticism, working with Tyler and providing opportunities for more physically based learning such as sports and outdoor work will give him an opportunity to channel his energies. Receiving praise for doing well will improve his self-esteem and lead to him feeling more able to trust other adults. Positive role models using male staff often succeed with children like Tyler.

Nurture groups

For some children and young people educational settings may use or have set up a nurture group as a means of supporting individuals who exhibit behavioural needs linked to issues surrounding their social and emotional development. Often such groups involve supporting children and young people who have damaged or insecure attachments with adults and their peers and as a result of this are vulnerable and therefore at risk of exclusion in an educational setting.

By using a Boxall Profile (Bennathan and Haskayne, 2007) settings can assess whether children and young people will need to be supported by a nurture group practitioner in a base room outside their normal classroom where they may be withdrawn for support. The Boxall Profile uses questionnaires to provide a means of assessing the negative and positive behaviours of children and young people who are displaying signs of social, emotional and behavioural difficulties (SEBD). Such an assessment can then be used to provide advice on how best to support and address any issue identified.

Often such children exhibit behavioural issues centred on:

- being quiet and withdrawn with poor relationships with adults and their peers;

- having friendship difficulties – keeping/making friends, accepting the rule of a game and sharing;

- finding it hard to listen to others or join in;

- having a low self-esteem;

- being disruptive towards others and whilst in lessons;

- bullying others.

Nurture groups often provide a time-limited intervention for children outside their normal school-based routines, supplying those development experiences often missed by the pupil which may have limited their ability to make trusting relationships with grownups or to relate appropriately to their peers. The success of this work centres on the positive, supportive role models that the staff can bring to these children and young people's lives. Role modelling and observations of these positive relationships provide an opportunity to practise and develop behaviours that are more socially acceptable, with such work being reinforced by the development of language and communications skills within the individual.

Examples of the type of successful strategies employed by nurture group practitioners may include having a clear start to the day by having the practitioner in the room which has been prepared prior to the pupil's arrival with a range of activities that they can choose from. Given the sometimes anxious state of some individuals on their arrival, this structure and its choice provides comfort and reassurance to the child or young person supporting their mental health and well-being. The structure and activities also prepares them for reintegration into a school day in the future when they re-join their class. Breakfast, or the creation of food, may help create a positive attachment to a member of staff as well as providing a loving and caring relationship where trust is formed. This can also enhance communications skills such as waiting to take one's turn as well as social skills such as sitting down and using cutlery. Something so simple may be alien to a child with a chaotic home life. Circle time may also be used to stimulate discussion and to build up their self-esteem. Personal literacy and numeracy targets will also be worked on during their day so as to reduce the likelihood of disruptive behaviour due to frustration of not being able to succeed in a whole class setting. Praise and rewards will be used to build up self-esteem as well as consistent and clear boundaries helping to reinforce the need to behave in an acceptable manner. Nurture groups generally end the day on a positive note or by reinforcing the knowledge that a fresh start is always available the next day. Using achievement books provides a means of sharing their achievements with their parent or carer. This can be a positive talking point for them, as well as a recognition that doing well is key in building self-esteem.

The organisation, commitment and work of nurture groups within educational settings has been investigated and recognised by organisations such as Ofsted:

> Nurture interventions involves a considerable investment from schools in terms of finance, time, planning and resources and staff training. However, the survey illustrates that, when successful, the impact on young children and their families can be highly significant and far-reaching.

> (Ofsted, 2011, p5)

CASE STUDY: CATHERINE

Catherine recently joined our school in Year 4 and was in foster care having been removed from her mother's and her stepfather's care due an abusive home setting. She was placed in kinship foster care with her gran and was very frightened, anxious and withdrawn when she joined us. She was very reluctant to share with others in her class and would often shout at them or not let them speak. She would often snatch things off them when they were working. Her vocabulary and social skills were very limited and her self-esteem was low. Catherine's gran was keen to help and support the school to help with Catherine's difficulties, health and well-being.

Case study reflections

- How might a nurture group benefit Catherine?
- What might a nurture group do to involve and support Catherine's gran?
- What aspects of Catherine's development will the staff at the nurture group have to focus on?

So what did the school do to help Catherine?

By working with the school SENCo and having her needs assessed using a Boxall Profile, it was agreed that Catherine should join the school's nurture group to help with her issues. This group provided an ideal opportunity for Catherine to feel supported and served as a place where caring relationships could be established. Catherine was invited to take turns in circle time activities, if she felt comfortable to do so, which was used to build up her self-esteem as well as creating opportunities for her to sit down and share and develop aspects of herself. When taking part in cooking activities she started to create more positive relationships and learnt when cooking with others to engage in conversation and social skills such as taking turns and listening and waiting. Catherine was encouraged to develop a sense of pride and achievement which helped her with her self-esteem. Catherine took the cakes she baked home so that the skills she had practised in her group could be reinforced when sharing them with her gran. This involved her gran in her school life and provided another opportunity for praise to be given to Catherine for her achievements. After a term in the nurture group it was felt that due to Catherine's progress she could return to some activities in her class.

If this topic has been new to you and you wish to gain more useful advice and support regarding nurture groups, you can visit the Nurture Group Network website at **www.nurturegroups.org/about-nurture**.

KEY REFLECTIONS

- How might a setting assess the SEBD of an individual?
- What behaviours might a child or young person with SEBD difficulties exhibit in their setting?
- How might a nurture group support and lead to the successful reintegration of an individual who has SEBD difficulties back into their classroom setting?

Special Educational Needs and Disability Code of Practice

For some children or young people exhibiting behavioural difficulties, it is important to realise that such issues may not always be caused by SEND issues linked to their mental health and well-being. However, when mental health and well-being issues are leading to consistent disruptive behaviour and this is having a direct impact upon the social, emotional and academic life of an individual, the setting must follow statutory regulations to support such children and young adults through the Special Educational Needs and Disability Code of Practice (SEND CoP; DfE, 2015). A range of mental health issues may require that special provision is made available. For some children, behavioural conditions such as autism spectrum disorder (ASD) will be identified and treated for prolonged periods of time using medication in their setting as part of a clinical diagnosis and treatment plan. However, for other children and young people, their behavioural difficulties may be linked to environmental or contextual issues with these conditions presenting themselves over a sustained or more sporadic or temporary length of time. However, whatever the cause or type of behaviour difficulties, such as aggression or anxiety, an individual may exhibit such conditions, which will no doubt impact upon the child's academic and social progress in schools with pupils often failing to meet their own rates of previous progress or to match up to that of their peers. Given such underperformance or types of trigger for unacceptable behaviours the educational setting will have a duty to support such children and young adults under the SEND CoP (DfE, 2015). This will be deemed as 'SEND Support' once parents have been consulted and their agreement secured for this intervention. It is important to remember that the SEND CoP (DfE, 2015) legislation clearly states that the majority of individuals (except for a limited number of exceptions) given their SEND must be accommodated and educated in the mainstream setting with this being accomplished by the important involvement of their carers or parents.

The SEND CoP (DfE, 2015, p98) clearly outlines in one of its broad areas of need that schools may need to support children who can be identified to have 'social, emotional and mental health' needs. This can include children who are withdrawn or isolated, as well as exhibiting disruptive, challenging or disturbing behaviours, with these conditions in some cases being linked to underlying issues such as anxiety, depression, self-harm, substance abuse, eating disorders or physical symptoms that cannot be explained. Other conditions covered by this category include attention deficit disorder, attention deficit hyperactivity disorder or attachment disorders.

The Code of Practice (DfE, 2015) advocates that most children with special educational needs should be supported in their education through extra help provided in the educational setting and that they should be provided with high quality, differentiated provision in order to support the individual which will be co-ordinated by the school's special educational needs coordinator (SENCo). This person, often a teacher within the school, will be responsible for working with other teachers and parents to ensure that pupils with SEND get the appropriate level of support and the help that they need at school.

Such a SEND-based approach will be supported by the use of information such as school attainment, information gathered by other health and/or social care professionals, attendance data and by the knowledge gained by the setting pastoral support system. Depending on the severity of need, different levels of support may be provided through 'waves' of intervention or an Education, Health and Care (EHC) Plan. However, the success of any such support must be underpinned by a personalised assessment of the child's or young person's needs.

Through the use of 'Wave 1' interventions, class-based strategies to support improvements in behaviour can be used, this also being known as 'Quality First Teaching' (QFT). This may include class-based strategies such as visual timetables, group work to promote speaking and listening skills, the use of opportunities for personalised learning, the use of rewards and sanctions stickers and behavioural charts, for example, the use of zone boards. Such work will be complemented by the use of the SEAL programme to promote such positive behaviours both in the school and at home. This will help the development of emotional literacy so that individuals can communicate feelings, to help them manage their anger, anxiety and fear, as well as providing strategies for controlling their emotions. If individuals fail to make progress the SEND intervention may graduate onto a 'Wave 2' intervention.

'Wave 2' interventions will involve the identification of additional time-limited provision which may take the form of a small group intervention so as to enable pupils to make greater social and emotional progress and to help the child work at their age-related expectations. Such interventions may take the form of supporting social skills to help them in managing peer relationships, for example programmes such as socially speaking or help with their self-esteem through SEAL resources such as 'Good to be me'. If such interventions are unsuccessful then pupils can progress onto 'Wave 3' interventions which can include the school involving specialists or outside agencies such as educational psychologists or CAMHS, to help identify and support such settings. Highly personalised interventions used in Wave 3 programmes that may help with behaviour can include counselling sessions or the use of trained bereavement counsellor from organisations such as Winston's Wish. Interventions from trained individuals in the promotion of mindfulness can also help individuals manage issues around anger, stress and anxiety. For more information with regard to how literacy may be supported using a 'wave model' of intervention you can visit **www.interventionsfor literacy.org.uk/home/parents/sen-provision**.

Whatever the child's behaviourial needs or intervention programme, teaching assistants/learning support assistants/higher learning teaching assistants or school learning mentors can provide a vital academic and emotional support, wherever the child is placed on the SEND code of practice. Given their detailed knowledge of the child or young adult these professionals can often:

- effectively help plan and deliver effective interventions programmes;

- recognise and intervene before a brewing issue escalates;

- take the class so that an issue can be dealt with effectively by the teacher without learning time being affected;

- use their relationship with the child to promote their co-operation when needed.

For some children with complex education, health and care needs which are impacting on the individual's behaviour, the school-based SEND support may prove insufficient and additional provision can be provided to support the child through an Education, Health and Care (EHC) Plan. To obtain such support a detailed assessment to identify the child's special educational needs (if requested by the parents or educational setting) will be carried out. This will involve the educational setting evidencing the need and support given to the child as well as gaining information to support this application from individuals involved with the child or young person. This will include individuals such as the parent, teacher, educational psychologist, health professional/child's doctor, physiotherapist or health visitor and any social services based professionals. If successfully granted an EHC Plan will provide additional support from the local authority (LA) to enable the successful support of this child or young adult's needs. Through an agreed personal budget, families and the educational setting can decide and agree how provision is arranged and how the budget for a child/young person is to be spent.

When working with some children and young people a Family Common Assessment Framework (FCAF) can provide a strategy to help support an individual's needs. Though an FCAF is a voluntary process, it will allow the lead professional to bring together other support agencies such as health visitor, children's centre worker, teacher or school nurse so that they can help identify how a child or young person can receive the right support at an early stage before their needs increase. An action plan is then agreed to make sure that the individual can get the right sort of help to support their behaviour.

 KEY REFLECTIONS

- How might behavioural issues relate to the SEND CoP?
- How might the 'waves' of interventions support individuals with behavioural issues?
- How might teaching assistants and outside agencies, rather than just teachers, support the provision of children and young people with behavioural issues?

 CASE STUDY: AKIO

Akio is currently in a Year 2 class. His mother is now really struggling with his anger at home and is often coming to the class teacher at her wits' end saying that she can no longer cope. Father is no longer living with the family though he is involved in Akio's life and he is concerned his mental health issues are somehow related to his son's mental state of mind. Akio's behaviour is deteriorating in class with him shouting out constantly and hurting others when on the carpet. His constant mood swings and low self-esteem are now impacting on his progress. He is currently receiving Wave 2 support in terms of small group interventions to support his learning and behaviour by the class teaching assistant.

Case study reflections

- What risk factors does Akio have?
- How might the school continue to support Akio?

Since Akio's mother is engaging with the school they certainly should, given his issues, be looking to support him by moving onto Wave 3 levels of support. They could involve other agencies in helping to support his mother and father, Akio and the setting in dealing with his behavioural issues.

This support may come through a referral to CAMHS or a child psychologist for an assessment alongside support from the school nurse and the family's GP. Interventions may include: provision of parenting/family-based interventions or possibly some one-to-one therapy for Akio in the form of counselling or cognitive behaviour therapy. The school could deploy a learning mentor, if they have one, to support Mum by providing a first point of contact for her to share her concerns in school. Certainly some Wave 3 interventions such as 'socially speaking' may help him consider his actions when on the carpet or when learning. If both Mum and Dad were willing, an FCAF certainly could progress a shared assessment of need and an action plan for how the agencies could work together to help support Akio and his parents. If Mum and Dad were willing they could have some family support through a health professional to help them with their current difficulties and help them to understand and manage Akio's behaviour at home. In the long term, if things continue to deteriorate despite the support offered, an EHC Plan could be applied for.

Levels of support

It is important to realise that though some issues around mental health and well-being are of ongoing concern, such issues can be triggered by a critical incident such as an unexpected death in the school. If this is the case, not only will perhaps the pupils be affected but if it is the loss of a close member of staff, the remaining staff and teaching team will be severely affected. These events are hard to plan for, but if this is the case support services may be accessed from voluntary organisations such as the Teacher Support Network (24 hours a day, throughout the year, support line) or through statutory agencies who can offer support such as bereavement counselling. Some educational settings will employ their own school-based counsellors or fund some shared arrangement with other schools. Such professionals will be important to support every aspect of an educational setting's mental health and emotional well-being, and their work may be supported by interventions such as play therapy or art/music therapy.

However, sometimes, despite high levels of school support, some children and young adults with high risk factors may find their mental health and well-being issues lead to behavioural issues and can ultimately lead to either temporary or permanent exclusion. Given a permanent exclusion, most pupils will end up attending a Pupil Referral Unit (PRU) which (under section 19 of the Education Act 1996) exists to provide education to children who are of compulsory school age who are unable to attend a maintained school for reasons of sickness, exclusion or other issues. A PRU will provide an academic education, and specially trained staff are on hand to respond to children's needs and to deal with and support any arising challenges to education.

 KEY REFLECTIONS

- What are some of the key risk factors that can trigger behavioural issues around mental health and well-being?
- What strategies can educational professionals put in place to support the range of behavioural needs encountered?

(Continued)

(Continued)

- What outside agency support is available to support a school in addressing behavioural issues around mental health and well-being?
- What statutory requirements are placed on schools to support individuals who have behavioural issues?

CHAPTER SUMMARY

- A range of presenting behavioural issues can indicate a potential mental health and well-being problem.
- Schools have statutory duties to support and include pupils who have behavioural difficulties linked to their mental health and well-being needs.
- Appropriate supportive responses are crucial, including providing clear strategies to support individuals both in the classroom and through a range of provision linked to education, thus providing a climate in which children and young people with behavioural issues can flourish.
- Outside agencies can support teaching staff, schools and leaders who have concerns about children and young people's behaviour.
- The professionals who work in their settings have a clear role to play in identifying and supporting children with behavioural issues.

FURTHER READING

Blakemore, S.J. (2012) The mysterious workings of the adolescent brain: www.ted.com/talks/sarah_jayne_blakemore_the_mysterious_workings_of_the_adolescent_brain.

Bombèr, L.M. (2011) *What About Me? Inclusive Strategies to Support Pupils with Attachment Difficulties Make it Through the School Day*. London: Worth Publishing.

Geddes, H. (2005) *Attachment in the Classroom: The Links Between Children's Early Experience, Emotional Well-being and Performance in School*. London: Worth Publishing.

Goepel, J., Childerhouse, H. and Sharpe, S. (2015) *Inclusive Primary Teaching*. 2nd edition. Northwich: Critical Publishing.

Marshall, N. (2014) *The Teacher's Introduction to Attachment: Practical Essentials for Teachers, Carers and School Support Staff*. London: Jessica Kingsley Publishers.

Rogers, B. (2011) *Classroom Behaviour: A Practical Guide to Effective Teaching, Behaviour Management and Colleague Support*. 3rd edition. London: SAGE.

━━ REFERENCES ━━

Bennathan, M. and Haskayne, M. (2007) *What is the Boxall Profile and how effective is it?* Available at: http://schools.bracknell-forest.gov.uk/sites/default/files/assets/what-is-the-boxall-profile-and-how-effective-is-it.pdf (accessed 11 October 2016).

Cole, T. (2015) *Mental health difficulties and children at risk of exclusion from schools in England: A review from an educational perspective of policy, practice and research, 1997 to 2015.* Available at www.education.ox.ac.uk/wordpress/wp-content/uploads/2015/02/MENTAL-HEALTH-AND-EXCLUSION-FINAL-DIGITAL-13-06-15.pdf (accessed 23 September 2016).

Department for Education (DfE) (2012) *Behaviour and discipline in schools: Guidance for governing bodies.* Crown Copyright.

Department for Education (2015) *Special educational needs and disability code of practice: 0 to 25 years.* Available at: www.gov.uk/government/uploads/system/uploads/attachment_data/file/398815/SEND_Code_of_Practice_January_2015.pdf (accessed 26 August 2016).

Department for Education (2016a) *Behaviour and discipline in schools: Advice for headteachers and school staff.* Available at: www.gov.uk/government/uploads/system/uploads/attachment_data/file/488034/Behaviour_and_Discipline_in_Schools_-_A_guide_for_headteachers_and_School_Staff.pdf (accessed 20 August 2016).

Department for Education (2016b) *Mental health and behaviour in schools.* Available at: www.gov.uk/government/publications/mental-health-and-behaviour-in-schools–2 (accessed 12 September 2016).

Ofsted (2005) *Managing Challenging Behaviour.* London: Ofsted.

Ofsted (2009) *The Exclusion from School of Children Aged Four to Seven.* London: Ofsted.

Ofsted (2011) *Supporting children with challenging behaviours through a nurture group approach.* Available at: www.gov.uk/government/publications/supporting-children-with-challenging-behaviour (accessed 23 September 2016).

Schore, A. (2005) Attachment, affect regulation and the developing right brain: Linking development neuroscience to paediatrics. *Paediatrics in Review*, 26(6). London: The British Library.

Sellgren, K. (2013) 'Disruptive behaviour rising, teachers say'. *BBC News.* Available at: www.bbc.co.uk/news/education-21895705 (accessed 19 August 2016).

Steer, A. (2011) *Learning behaviours lessons learned: A review of behaviours standards and practices in our school.* Available at: www.educationengland.org.uk/documents/pdfs/2009-steer-report-lessons-learned.pdf (accessed on 22 August 2016).

Weare, K. (2015) *What Works in Promoting Social and Emotional Well-being and Responding to Mental Health Problems in School?* London: National Children's Bureau.

Young Minds (2016) *About self-esteem.* Available at: www.youngminds.org.uk/for_parents/whats_worrying_you_about_your_child/self-esteem/about_self-esteem (accessed 1 January 2016).

4
SELF-ESTEEM

Chapter objectives

By the end of this chapter you should be aware of:

- defining self-esteem;
- the impact of positive self-esteem on children;
- the impact of poor self-esteem on children;
- how self-esteem represents an aspect of the risk/resilience model;
- strategies that can support improving self-esteem both with children and young people and the school community.

Teachers' Standards

This chapter supports the development of the following Teachers' Standards:

TS1: Set high expectations which inspire, motivate and challenge pupils

- Establish a safe and stimulating environment for pupils, rooted in mutual respect.

TS7: Manage behaviour effectively to ensure a good and safe learning environment

- Manage classes effectively, using approaches which are appropriate to pupils' needs in order to involve and motivate them.

TS8: Fulfil wider professional responsibilities

- Develop effective professional relationships with colleagues, knowing how and when to draw on advice and specialist support.
- Communicate effectively with parents with regard to pupils' achievements and well-being.

Introduction

This chapter will focus on the crucial role that the development of self-esteem can play in the lives of children and young people. It will examine how a developing sense of 'self' mediates the creation of self-esteem and the important role that social relationships and significant risk factors can have on its development. The link between 'self-efficacy' and self-esteem will be examined, along with its role in the feelings created towards a child's level of achievement. Consideration will be given to how positive and negative self-esteem may manifest itself in children's actions and influence their beliefs regarding their own abilities. Finally, the chapter will also focus on what may be done in a school setting to promote positive self-esteem and to support its promotion within members of the school community.

What is self-esteem?

Self-esteem is how we think about ourselves and is reflective of our emotional evaluation of self-worth; this concept begins to grow and develop in a child's early years. An individual with positive self-esteem will feel they are a good person, deserving of love and support, who can be successful. Low self-esteem leads to feelings of not being good enough, undeserving of love or support and a feeling that things will work out badly (Young Minds, 2016). Low self-esteem was the second highest reason for calls to ChildLine in 2014–15, accounting for more than 35,000 calls, citing children's struggles with friendship, impossible aspirations and the hazards of social media as contributing factors (NSPCC, 2015). 'Self' is the product of relationships with others according to what is happening and being experienced at the time. Nick Luxmoore (2008) also discusses how saying 'hello' sounds simple but that it is the foundation from which a sense of self develops. This reminds us that we all exist in relation to others and with a sense of self developing through others' response and recognition of us. This is also in-keeping with the role and importance of 'connectedness' cited as a resilience factor, in relation to school experiences (Weare, 2015).

All of us are born into a context of relationships, as well as what is happening within that context at the time. The development of babies' brains is influenced by relationships with other important people in their life. Becoming a 'person' involves a large investment by others early in life, not only from family and friends but also communities and schools. Within any relationship, we will look to others for messages that provide us with a sense of our worth as a person. From this, an emerging sense of self becomes reflected back to us through the eyes and minds of others. As Music (2011, p7 and 24) describes:

> a *person's sense of self arises from being in the minds of others, without which it simply does not develop ... and that one's sense of self is socially and co-constructed ... human life develops from the delicate interplay of nature and nurture, the meeting of a bundle of inherited potentials and the cultural, social and personal influences of the adults in an infant's life.*

Positive self-esteem also has close links to, and can influence a child's feelings of, actual and perceived competence, or 'self-efficacy' (Bandura, 1977, 1989). This is the belief that we are capable of doing something and that we can influence events that affect our lives. A child's level of self-efficacy can vary, but it continues to evolve throughout childhood. A child with high self-efficacy will be more optimistic, less anxious and have a higher level of problem-solving skills, with the ability to persevere in times of difficulty, focusing less on the possibility of failure (Plummer and Harper, 2007). This is a concept that requires nurturing throughout childhood, especially within schools, as enabling a child to develop a sense of mastery and the ability to overcome a challenge will also, simultaneously, develop positive self-esteem. Thus demonstrating that 'core self-evaluations' such as self-esteem and self-efficacy do not operate in isolation but can overlap with other dimensions of the 'self' (Bono and Judge, 2003).

Luxmoore (2008) makes the case for the 'self' being socially constructed and therefore with hope for repair, noting that 'self' is not a thing in itself but a way of understanding and describing our experience. This is in-keeping with risk and resilience theories as being a dynamic and evolving process. If relationships get off to a poor start and are damaged there is opportunity for reparation through future positive relationships. Self-esteem is an aspect of human development which is very sensitive to the quality of other relationships and so has a capacity for new possibilities and positive development. Relationships continue to be important and are at the heart of well-being and self-esteem. These develop in the school environment with friends, peers and teachers (The Children's Society, 2015).

There will be many children and young people in schools who have experienced their own 'self' (and thus their self-esteem) being adversely affected. This will be especially relevant for children in the care system. There were 70,440 looked after children at 31 March 2016, an increase of 1 per cent in the past year, and an increase of 8 per cent compared to 2011. This rise over time reflects the higher number of children starting to be looked after than those ceasing to be, so there will be significant proportions of these children in classrooms (Williams, 2016; DfE, 2016). Consider the numbers of these looked after children who will be in schools and who will all have experienced loss, trauma and significant life events on multiple levels. In addition, many other children may also have had similar experiences, all of which impact on 'self' and identity. Young Minds (2014, cited in Weare, 2015, p8) reported that in an average classroom ten young people will have experienced parents separating, eight will have experienced severe physical violence, sexual abuse or neglect, one will have experienced the death of a parent and seven will have been bullied.

Additionally, it is important to note that in the United Kingdom we have some of the poorest overall well-being of children in the world despite living in a materially resource-rich society. The UNICEF (2011) Report Card 11: *An Overview of Child Well-being in Rich Countries* found that we rank 16th out of 29 countries. The five dimensions researched included: material well-being, health and safety, education, behaviours and risks, and housing and environment (follow this link for more detail: **www.unicef.org.uk/Images/Campaigns/FINAL_RC11-ENG-LORES-fnl2.pdf**).

This was, however, an improvement on the earlier UNICEF Report Card 7 (2007) where the United Kingdom was ranked last out of 21 countries. A study by the Jacobs Foundation conducted between 2013 and 2015 looked at 8-year-olds in 16 countries over four continents. It examined children's well-being from their own perspectives. Overall, the report showed children in the United Kingdom have a low sense of well-being. In all the domains assessed, the United Kingdom was at the lower end of all other countries (Rees et al., 2016). Seemingly, we have some of the unhappiest children in the world. It may also be important to consider the different educational models, particularly in Sweden, compared to the UK. Findings in 'The Good Childhood Report 2015' (The Children's Society, 2015) indicated children struggle with feelings and perceptions of themselves and about life at school and suggested this was an area for future prioritisation. Some of the other reasons cited are school pressures and stress from the increasing amount of testing and exams together with peer pressure about looking a particular way. Positive self-esteem and happiness are very closely linked, as are poor self-esteem and unhappiness.

KEY REFLECTIONS

- How would you define self-esteem?
- What part can relationships play in the construction of self-esteem?
- How might levels of self-esteem manifest themselves in a child?

The importance of self-esteem

Self-esteem is a vital component to individuals and their lives since it affects their life choices and decision-making process. Children with high self-esteem are generally motivated and will seek to achieve well in life; whilst on the other hand children with lower self-esteem tend not to feel worthy and can lack the motivation to achieve.

Young Minds (2016) summarises positive self-esteem in children and young people as:

- having a positive image of oneself;
- being confident;
- making friends easily and not being anxious around new people;
- playing in groups or alone;
- trying and solving problems, but asking for help if necessary;
- taking pride in achievements;
- admitting mistakes and learning from them;
- trying new things and adapting to change.

Similarly poor self-esteem is summarised by Young Minds (2016) as:

- having a negative image of oneself and possibly feeling ugly, bad, unlikeable or stupid;
- having a lack of confidence;
- finding it hard to make and keep friends and feeling victimised by others;
- tending to avoid new things and finding change hard;
- an inability to deal well with failure;

- tending to put oneself down and say things such as: 'I am stupid' or 'I can't do that' (before trying);

- taking no pride in achievements and always thinking they could have done better;

- constantly comparing to peers in a negative way.

The importance of resilience

As the risk and resilience model will show, low self-esteem is one of the risk factors in the development of poor mental health whereas positive or high self-esteem acts as a protective factor to mental health. Children and young people with low self-esteem are at a higher risk of developing mental health problems over their life time.

Self-esteem was defined by Pearce (1993) as one of the protective factors in terms of the likelihood of developing mental health problems. Children with low self-esteem are more at risk of developing mental health problems (Young Minds, 2016). His risk and resilience model identified three areas of risk:

1. environmental/contextual;

2. the family;

3. the young person/child themselves.

Examples of risk include:

- negative experiences in the *environment* such as poverty, disaster, violence or being a refugee or asylum seeker;

- precipitating factors in the *family* such as early attachment difficulties, domestic abuse, parental conflict and parental mental illness;

- for the *young person*, areas of risk include neurodevelopmental difficulties and conditions (such as attention deficit hyperactivity disorder (ADHD) or autistic spectrum conditions (ASC)), low self-esteem, academic failure and poor school attendance, low IQ or learning difficulties, physical illness and genetic influences. Multiple family transitions can increase risk with a cumulative effect on educational achievement, behaviour and relationships in general.

Yet, in spite of major adversity, many young people and children cope well. The key is *resilience* which acts as a protective factor. Rutter (1985) and again later (2006) described this as a dynamic evolving process and not just about static factors. The model of risk and resilience is not based on risk and protective factors in themselves but rather on how they interact. The flip side is the consideration of resilience factors which mitigate the risk factors. Having and acquiring resilience skills acts as a protective factor, and these can include:

- secure attachments;

- positive self-esteem;

- social skills;

- familial compassion and warmth;

- family stability;

- social support systems that encourage personal development and coping skills;

- having a skill or a talent.

The emphasis is on the process of resilience across developmental pathways. Studies have led theorists to suggest that each child inherits characteristics which make them both vulnerable (risk factors) and resilient (protective factors). There is a complex interplay between risk factors and promoting resilience. Resilience effects are shaped by social context. So, for children and young people, this includes educational settings. Even high risk groups as suggested above are able to individually adapt and achieve against the odds and despite diversity (Rutter, 2012). A focus is often on risk or negative factors instead of positive attributes and resilience. In the following case study of Max, ADHD ticks a box as a risk factor but it is really important to know and practise re-framing ADHD as a positive factor. It is most likely Max will have boundless energy, which can be wearing for those around him, but he will always be keen on participating in events outside the classroom where he could potentially do well. A 'state of mind' and improved self-esteem can come about through experiencing successes.

Where protective and resilience factors can be accessed, resourced and utilised, they can act as an important counterbalance to risk factors (DfE, 2015). For example a child may be genetically predisposed to developing ADHD. There may be other family members with a diagnosis. With the combination of a poor environment in terms of abuse or attachment difficulties, the child may be at greater risk of developing ADHD (Music, 2011). Similarly, a young person may be genetically predisposed to clinical depression or psychosis, which does not in itself mean the condition will necessarily develop. But if there is a combination of other poor external factors and negative experiences as described above, depression, psychosis or other significant mental illness may emerge and develop into a clinical condition (Burton et al., 2014). Many children will experience an understandable knock to their self-esteem from these challenges; some are able to bounce back if there are other protective factors in place, or as Fuller (1998, p75) describes:

> Resilience is the happy knack of being able to bungy jump through the pitfalls of life.

Perhaps understandably, others will find this more difficult and prolonged (Young Minds, 2016).

Resilience is a process and construct of individuals, families and communities including schools, societies and groups. As Rutter (1987, cited in Werner and Smith, 2001, p3) describes, it is:

> the end product of buffering processes that do not eliminate risk and adverse conditions in life but allow the individual to deal with them effectively.

Schools have an important role and can offer opportunities for supporting, promoting and improving children's resilience by using strength-based approaches including positive praise and the use of circle time. Through these activities, schools have an important role in helping to reduce the risk of children developing mental health problems (DfE, 2015).

Alongside self-esteem, identifying a skill or a talent – also a protective factor – should not be under-estimated. Mo Farah, the Olympic champion, was a migrant from Somalia, escaping the civil war and arriving in London aged 8 and speaking very little English. His potential athletic talent was spotted by his PE teacher at school and the rest, as we know, is history. The story had the potential to be so different (Burton et al., 2014).

 CASE STUDY: MAX

Max is 8 and in Year 3 at primary school. Max has a diagnosis of ADHD, so he struggles with the 'triad of impairments' for ADHD, is easily distracted, finds it difficult to concentrate for very long and is sometimes impulsive. To support this, the school is trying to give him short tasks that have a clear structure and are differentiated to allow Max to succeed. At lunch time he finds it difficult to remain in the lunch queue so sometimes gets asked to keep still and stay in line by the dinner time staff and sometimes gets sent to the back of the queue if he doesn't comply. Max also finds staying on task difficult in class. There are 29 other children in class. Max has a teaching assistant to sup-port him. He is always pleased to receive praise and has some gold stars for being able to stay on task in class. Despite this support he sometimes gets into trouble with staff both in and outside the classroom. When this happens he can get very upset. Life at home for Max is also difficult at times. He has an older brother, Tom, who is 16 and also has ADHD. The family have recently lost their father from the family home as the relationship between Tom and Max's parents has ended after an acrimonious time. Max and his family live in a two bedroom flat on an inner-city estate. Mum has recently been diagnosed with clinical depression. A favourite time of the school day is outside play. Max gets on well with peers and has some good friendships. Max enjoys sports, particularly foot-ball. He attends after school football club and plays football on Saturdays at a local sports centre.

Given this scenario there are many risk factors that are linked to Max's issues.

- Environment: inner-city estate, two bedroom flat, outside access to play limited as there is no garden. Opportunities for play can be reduced in schools where there has been a reduction in playtimes.
- Family: acrimonious parental relationship, father has left so significant event and loss. Brother has ADHD. Mum has a diagnosed mental health disorder.
- Child: Max has a neurodevelopmental difficulty (ADHD). Max finds it difficult to deal with being told off at school, which is more frequent for Max perhaps compared to other children which could contribute to low self-esteem, together with other factors as above.

However, despite these risk factors there are several potential resilience factors, which can improve Max's self-esteem. These include:

- enjoying and being good at sport (football);
- having friendships;
- attending after school clubs and engaging at school;
- having quick thinking, boundless energy and an 'up for it' activist personality and attitude to life as results of his ADHD;
- home life for Max has the potential to settle down and be less acrimonious now the parents have separated.

(Continued)

(Continued)

The school is also trying to support Max by using different strategies such as focused tasks, the use of positive praise and the support of a teaching assistant. By encouraging Max to join the school football club, the school is enabling him to regularly taste success and feel positive about his achievements outside the classroom, which will lead to improved self-esteem.

KEY REFLECTIONS

- How can high and low levels of self-esteem be characterised in a child?
- What risk and resilience factors can impact upon self-esteem?
- How can resilience be promoted within schools?

The value of self-efficacy

As mentioned earlier, self-efficacy is closely linked with self-esteem and develops from experiences throughout a child's life. It is the belief the child or young person has that they can define a goal, persevere and see themselves as capable, and in this way self-efficacy provides the foundation for motivation, well-being and personal accomplishment. To build self-efficacy children and young people need opportunities to learn what their strengths are, helping to cultivate a belief that they can rely on these when facing a challenge. Within a whole school approach, children and young people need to feel they have influence, a 'voice' and involvement in decision-making about their learning, classroom and school life (Weare, 2015). Ultimately, the more a child or young person believes they can achieve, the more likely they are to generalise this to other areas of their lives, building self-efficacy in a wide range of activities.

The case study below helps to demonstrate the importance of positive, trusting and empowering relationships and how schools can play a part in developing a child/young person's sense of mastery and the ability to persevere in times of difficulty, building self-efficacy. This was a vulnerable young person in difficult circumstances, and the end of the story could easily have been very different.

CASE STUDY: BECKY

Becky is 11, of dual heritage ethnicity and is in Year 6. Her family life is difficult; a volatile relationship with an overpowering mother and an absent father. Becky's mother (Rosie) struggles with her own mental health and finds it very difficult to put the needs of her children before her own. Becky's three older half-siblings have left home and her younger brother was, in her words, 'just annoying'. She lives in a three bedroomed house in an inner-city estate. Becky has struggled with low mood and anxiety since Year 4.

Becky has very low self-esteem and self-efficacy and was identified for increased support at school. Her school is very supportive of her and she has a particularly strong relationship with the deputy head teacher who is supporting the family with other professionals under the Common Assessment Framework (Children's Workforce Development Council, 2009). Becky and her family's needs were listened to and further thought was given as to how to meet them more effectively. Becky enjoyed school, was determined to attend school as much as possible and do as well as she could with her upcoming Key Stage 2 SATs, demonstrating hope and resilience.

Within counselling sessions at school Becky was supported to explore past and present relationships, how trust had been built and broken and how this affected her self-esteem and self-efficacy. Becky was given responsibilities within the classroom – lunch time monitor with other pupils, supporting a reading group of younger pupils – to encourage her sense of self-worth. Becky was very keen on drama but did not have the confidence to take part in lunch time rehearsals. With the support of the deputy head teacher, Becky was encouraged to attend and watch rehearsals, with a view to building on this.

The family support worker enabled Rosie to seek her own counselling and to work with her, reflecting on her relationship with Becky and possible strategies that may support them during difficult periods. With this support and encouragement Becky is developing into a more confident and capable young person and has a degree of control of her life. She is developing a more secure attachment to Rosie and a better relationship with her younger brother. Becky has strategies in place to help her manage difficult feelings in relation to her low mood and anxiety, increasing her sense of mastery.

Becky is attending school regularly and her self-esteem and belief that she can achieve and overcome difficulties in her life (self-efficacy) has grown immensely.

Becky's case demonstrates the important role that relationships play with regards to the development of self-esteem and self-efficacy. Professionals within Becky's school, particularly the deputy head teacher and the school counsellor, play an important role in increasing Becky's motivation and personal achievement.

Case study reflections

- With regard to self-efficacy, what made the difference in Becky's case?
- What factors did relationships play in supporting Becky's self-esteem?
- How are factors in the classroom supporting Becky's self-esteem?

There are many factors that are making a difference for Becky.

- Verbal persuasion and constructive feedback (hearing positive feedback about the ability to accomplish a desirable activity): Becky is gaining this from the supportive professional relationships in her life, particularly the deputy head teacher, building her self-esteem through positive relationships with others. Hearing is believing!

- Performance accomplishments (successfully doing a desired activity): Becky is on track with her Key Stage 2 SATs targets and is relishing her increased responsibilities at school. She is developing a stronger attachment to Rosie. All Becky's accomplishments have led to a sense of mastery, which is influencing her perspective on her own abilities. Doing is believing!

- Physiological states (feelings about the behaviour): Through positive relationships with others and the opportunity to think about the past with the school counsellor, Becky has been enabled to build her confidence and begun to control her low mood and anxiety. In turn, this is increasing her mood and positively impacting on her self-efficacy beliefs. Feeling is believing!

- Vicarious experience (seeing someone model the desired activity): Becky is observing other pupils within the drama group, younger pupils in the reading mentoring activity and her mother Rosie. She is looking at others and observing how they manage and whether they succeed or not, which is increasing her belief that she can indeed master her own situation. Seeing is believing!

It is important to note that desired activities and constructive feedback should not be unrealistic or grandiose as this can give children and young people the perception that they can accomplish an activity that they may not have the skills or knowledge to tackle. If a child or young person is encouraged to make a change that they are not ready to attempt, there is a possibility they may fail, and this can mean they will be less likely to believe they can do it the next time, resulting in a diminished sense of self-efficacy. It is extremely important, therefore, that success in activities is within reach and feedback is appropriate. In Becky's case, being encouraged to watch drama activities initially and being fully supported within other responsibilities are slowly developing her confidence and self-belief, which will in turn feed into positive self-esteem and high self-efficacy.

Improving self-esteem both with children and young people within the school and its community

It is relevant to consider strategies for promoting resilience, and it has to be remembered that resilience can only develop through some exposure to risk or stress; as Rutter (1985) identified, resilience develops through this exposure occuring at a *manageable level of intensity* at developmental points where protective factors can operate. The major risk factors for children and young people tend to operate within chronic and transitional events such as continuing family conflict, chronic and persistent bullying, long-term poverty and multiple school and home changes. Children and young people seem to show greater resilience when faced with more single one-off acute risk and adversity events, such as bereavement (Coleman and Hagell, 2007). A good caregiving relationship can act as a protective factor and can mitigate other social and environmental factors such as poverty and disability. In addition, caregiving relationships for children and young people also include relationships in school communities, thus becoming an important and additional resource. Resilience can be learnt, grown and developed, which can be a challenge in an assessment-based society such as ours, as well as in our schools' current national curriculum demands. There is a balance to be sought between the role of play as an asset and important tool for social development and subsequent development of resilience, and the pressure to achieve academic results, especially in early years settings (Joslyn, 2016).

Highly targeted therapeutic and educational support is required for identified at risk groups including, for example, looked after children (Scholfield et al., 2012). When the term 'therapeutic' is considered, it is not only about its application in clinical and counselling work. It is also with reference to the importance of all relationships having a therapeutic element which therefore is a supportive relationship. All looked after children in schools should have a Personal Education Plan (PEP), although it is interesting to read in *Promoting the Education of Looked after Children* (DfE, 2014) that the focus is on behaviour and achievement and there is no mention of mental health, apart from a requirement to work with local CAMHS as necessary. This is curious as looked after children and care leavers have a five-fold increased risk of all the childhood mental, emotional and behavioural problems and a six- to seven-fold increased risk of conduct disorders (DoH, 2011). Alternatively, the Department for Education's *Mental Health and Behaviour in Schools* (2015) guidance does not specifically consider and focus on looked after children as being at risk of mental ill health, which is also surprising.

A school's role

Promoting resilience and building self-esteem to prevent mental health issues in schools is a key area of focus for teachers and educational professionals. Weare (2015) highlights that the real benefits for schools can be seen through 'a whole school evidence informed approach' where a consistent group of approaches, programmes and interventions are designed and adopted so that all parts of the school work collaboratively towards building a safe and supportive school environment. When considering what 'good mental health' looks like the Mental Health Foundation (2002) state that a child would have the ability:

- to develop psychologically, emotionally, intellectually and spiritually;

- to initiate, develop and sustain mutually satisfying personal relationships;

- to become aware of others and empathise with them.

Therefore, building on this from a whole school approach perspective, teachers need to think about the class and wider school environment. Does it build a sense of connectedness and purpose where all emotions and feelings are supported through a culture of warmth and respect? How are being and feeling differently celebrated?

There are a number of approaches, programmes and interventions that can be initiated which focus on the teaching of social and emotional skills, and which in turn help develop positive school environments. It has been shown that these programmes, which help children understand the challenges associated with growing up, transitions in life (such as Key Stages and schools) and change (such as separation, divorce and bereavement), can build resilience which may prevent the development of mental health problems in later life. Resilience is being able to cope with difficult situations, and a child needs to able to believe in their ability to cope through a positive image of themselves which can be developed through the delivery of high quality programmes of social and emotional skills interventions.

One proposed structured programme in school could follow the WAVE model of intervention as supported by the revised SEND Code of Practice (DoH, 2014).

Wave 1	**Effective whole school framework for promoting emotional well-being and mental health** Quality first teaching of social and emotional skills to all children through PSHE-type programmes.
Wave 2	**Skills-focused interventions** Small group SEAL for children who need help to develop social and emotional skills.
Wave 3	**Therapeutic interventions** Individual and small groups. Complementary to SEAL.

All interventions would need to be informed by the evidence available through research, and mindful of a multi-professional approach to practice in order for them to be successful and have an impact on children and families.

Schools can play a central role in supporting educational resilience given the number of hours and length of time children spend in school. Educational resilience is not only about academic and educational attainment but is also about important relationships and social skills learnt in the process. This acts as a stabilising influence particularly for vulnerable children (Joslyn, 2016).

In order to support children in a variety of educational settings, Newman (2004, p14) also suggests a three-point strategy approach to promoting resilience within children.

Strategy 1	Reduce the child's exposure to risk though such means as providing school meals to support a child's life, or attendance at an after school club for children with no alternative but to play on the street.
Strategy 2	Interrupt the chain reaction of negative events; if one risk factor increases others will probably follow.
Strategy 3	Offer the child or young person positive experiences, thus providing ways of enhancing self-esteem and developing relationships with positive adults.

Alongside such an approach, a school may employ a strategy to help promote aspects of positive self-esteem, as outlined in the following section.

Personal, social, health and economic (PSHE)

Teaching children about mental health and emotional well-being should form part of a structured and personalised personal, social, health and economic (PSHE) curriculum in order to ensure that it proves an effective vehicle to embed core skills across all areas of educational experience and is not viewed as a 'bolt on' topic or theme. These sessions need to be tailored to the needs and age of the children in your class but a whole school approach of key messages is vital – that children are provided with the knowledge, language, understanding and confidence to seek help when needed and to ask questions about mental health without fear of stigmatism or bullying.

A graduated approach to PSHE education as a whole school is vital. With younger children work begins on 'developing oneself', focusing on self-awareness, self-concept, self-efficacy and self-belief.

An effective way to do this is through the development of emotional literacy through the use of story books. Stories and storytelling help children to develop emotional literacy, to make sense of their world and appreciate different points of view. It enables children to develop social relationships through an experiential, familiar and safe learning approach and start to develop skills such as empathy, negotiation, compassion and difference, an understanding of what is right and wrong, kind and unkind.

The Department for Education worked with the PSHE Association to improve the quality of teaching about mental health, and in spring 2015 the PSHE Association launched new guidance and primary and secondary lesson plans for schools on preparing to teach about mental health and emotional well-being under three core themes of 'health and well-being', 'relationships' and 'living in the wider world'.

Key issues included in these lesson plans are:

- Why it is important to teach about mental health and emotional well-being.

- Building teaching about mental health into a planned PSHE programme.

- Promoting well-being and resilience from an early age.

- Ensuring teaching is appropriate to the age and maturity of pupils.

- Key principles in teaching about mental health and emotional well-being safely and confidently.

- Using visitors to the classroom to support lessons.

- Addressing challenging mental health issues such as eating disorders, self-harm and suicide.

Good practice: promoting positive mental health

The use of feedback boxes allows pupils to share a problem anonymously in the 'bullying box', or something good that another pupil did in the 'praise box'. These are sometimes managed by the PSCHE (personal, social, citizenship and health education) co-ordinator, who may choose to file some comments and will pass safeguarding concerns on to the relevant staff member to follow up. This anonymous sharing allows teachers to pick up on common worries and problems which can then be discussed in weekly circle time sessions before they grow into more serious well-being or mental health risks. The teacher leads the discussion in a calm and respectful environment which allows the whole class to think together about what is happening without being judgemental or singling out the individuals involved. Reports from the boxes may also lead to referrals to Place2Be or CAMHS as well as other school-based interventions such as lunch time nurture clubs.

Social and emotional aspects of learning (SEAL)

The SEAL initiative (DfES, 2005) provided schools with a practical resource of learning opportunities to help develop social, emotional and behavioural skills through a whole school approach. As with the PSHE Association framework, SEAL built on a spiral curriculum delivery through a themed approach which could be adapted and personalised to fit the needs of individual classes and children. The development of a skills- and values-based approach was core to this, which was reinforced in classroom-based activities, whole school assemblies and links to home and the community. Although these resources are now no longer freely available and have been archived, many schools still use these approaches in their PSHE and circle time activities and they are also used for professional development training for staff.

This work was originally promoted by the research of individuals such as Goleman (1996), linked to the notion of emotional intelligence and was promoted by the government in publications such as DfES (2005a) 'Social and Emotional Aspects of Learning (SEAL): Improving behaviour, improving learning' and DfES (2005b) 'Excellence and enjoyment: Social and emotional aspects of learning'. Since the SEAL resources contained materials at their core which were designed to offer a selection of learning opportunities to achieve specific learning outcomes in the classroom, they can still provide advice and support for aiding the development of a child's self-esteem.

Materials linked to DfES (2005b) provide some excellent activities for helping children to develop an improved sense of self through the development of self-awareness. As DfES (2005b, p40) notes:

> Self-awareness enables children to have some understanding of themselves. They know how they learn, how they relate to others, what they are thinking and what they are feeling.

The materials linked to 'knowing myself' are particularly useful when considering how an individual can accept themselves for who and how they are, and in helping some individuals to be able to recognise when goals are hard to achieve. The unit linked to 'understanding my feelings' can help pupils recognise when they can become overwhelmed by their feelings and that it is all right to have feelings, but it is not all right to behave in any way they feel appropriate. 'Managing feelings' provides a range of strategies to recognise and accept feelings as well as managing and dealing with feelings.

Alongside SEAL materials, class-based strategies which involve listening to the child and praising them for their effort will provide one means by which to promote a child's self-esteem. However, try to avoid generic praise – be specific and descriptive, show children by what is said that you value them and their efforts too.

Always try and make certain that pupils taste success by setting achievable targets. Encourage a child through class-based opportunities to show their worth to the class. Ask them to talk about something they are knowledgeable about and successful in, or ask them to support their peers in a subject strength they have. Remember all pupils have their own strengths and weaknesses, so avoid comparing children since it can lead to unrealistic expectations and often the propagation of failure.

Circle time

Circle time was originally developed by Jenny Mosley in order to promote a respect for the individual as a whole and uses numerous practical activities for developing the whole person and their feelings of well-being (Mosley, 2001). Circle time sessions can also provide a possible vehicle for classroom delivery of the SEAL curriculum, as highlighted earlier. It centres on promoting positive relationships whilst seeking to nurture a sense of personal positivity and responsibility for others

(Mosley, 2004). Circle time allows the school and its pupils to experience a supportive environment in which social, emotional and behavioural skills can be developed.

Circle time allows participants (usually sitting in a circle) to exchange ideas and feelings linked to a variety of issues important to the child along with behavioural and emotional items. The teacher who is involved in these sessions is there to facilitate the discussions and to provide activities to encourage participants to feel that their contributions are valued and included. Linked to circle time are what are called 'golden rules' which are displayed around the school to remind pupils of the agreed principles for positive aspects of social and moral behaviour. For example these might include 'we do not hurt people's feelings'.

Through a supportive developmental framework of games circle time allows the pupils to consider aspects of their moral development involving their ideas supported by their peers. Games can include:

- Asking each child to choose a positive adjective to describe themselves and others as the game moves around the circle.

- Scenarios such as 'You see a child sitting on their own in the playground. They are upset by comments made by others about their football ability. What do you do?' helps to encourage pupils to think about the feelings of others and how they can promote a positive feeling of self-worth.

Working with parents

A school is often made aware of a child's low self-esteem as evidenced in the way they respond to praise and behave in school. Given this, the school should seek to work with the parents so as to try and promote improvements in a child's self-esteem both inside and outside of school.

At a school level, remember that positive relationships with children are key to positive behaviour and regular attendance. Also remember that children behave well when they feel valued and that they belong, and that the school should try to create opportunities for children to experience and/or feel confident in a positive relationship with an adult. This will take time and may need to involve others in the process, such as the parents.

Contact with parents to discuss the school's concerns regarding a child's self-esteem can be made both formally on occasions, such as parents' evening, or just when talking to a parent about a child's day when they are picked up. If this is to be a positive meeting it is important that whenever this is done, the member of staff makes certain that the parent does not in any way feel blamed or patronised regarding the child's behaviour. However, it is important that the parent is provided with help, support and strategies to deal with any behaviour at home both in a consistent and positive way.

Such conversations will ensure that strategies and approaches used in school can form part of what is an agreed united approach between home and school when trying to make inroads into this aspect of a child's well-being. This may also form the basis of a support package for parents, helping them to promote positive parenting and attitudes at home. Remember that for some parents they too may not have had positive experiences when they were young, with parents undermining their own feeling of self-worth. Given this, schools need to work with parents to make them also feel accepted and valued.

Strategies that can be employed both in school and at home

Identifying where the problem lies

Since children with poor self-esteem may find it difficult to articulate their feelings, try not to question them too much about why they are being negative. Often the child will not be able to pin an exact reason on their feelings. Just try and gently, in conversation, ask questions such as 'are you sure you are all right?' or 'if you want to tell me about your day, or the reason for your feelings, I am keen to listen'.

Trying and acknowledge that we cannot all be good at everything, all the time

For the child, feelings of being useless at their work are very much real, so you should listen to how the child feels but acknowledge that it is fine to feel this way and it is not uncommon to get cross, angry or sad from time to time. Tell them about moments you have struggled with issues to help them realise that it can happen to adults as well as children. If it is another child in the class that is denting the child's self-esteem, consider getting the child to think about negative points the other child may have as well as their positive aspects. This way the child can see that the other child may appear confident but has items they may feel vulnerable about, even though it is not shown. Try and to get to know the child's hopes and fears in a typical day and see if you can find a way to empathise with what the child is saying so you can support them more fully.

Concentrating on the positive points of the child

If a child is unhappy or upset try and talk to them at an appropriate moment about what the issues are that are upsetting them. Try not to probe for answers if the child is not forthcoming. Give them space and time to open up. Try not to get cross in these situations or criticise or blame the child. This will not help the situation and may even prove more problematic in the future. Remember to praise the child for their own unique positive strengths. Avoid comparisons with siblings or other pupils since this may lead to resentment or the child not being able to compete with them.

Positive parenting

It is important that you help parents to make every effort to praise their child when they have done well or tried hard. Little things will start having an impact upon self-esteem, for example thanking them for tidying their bag away or hanging their coat up when they come into the house. If a parent is finding it difficult to accept the child's behaviour, try and encourage them to make certain that the child sees and hears that it is the behaviour they do not like but not the child by using comments such as 'I like you but I do not like that behaviour'.

Teacher's self-esteem

Teachers often reflect on their own role in supporting a child with issues relating to self-esteem and often do not realise how these form part of being an effective teacher as outlined by Part B of the

Teachers' Standards (2014). However, in order for you to be effective when doing your job, you too must have high levels of self-esteem in order that you act in a confident, relaxed and respectful manner towards the children in your school. A teacher's self-esteem may be influenced by many factors such as feelings of inadequacy when dealing with school-based issues or due to their own personal lives. The question that must be asked, therefore, is 'who is looking after the self-esteem of the teaching workforce in the school?' Authors such as Mosley (2001) have advocated that there is a need to build positive self-esteem within the teaching workforce and that it may be assessed when examining the responses to set questions such as 'do you worry about your work when you are not in school?' Research by Weare (2015) notes that it is important that staff's successes and achievements are celebrated, but that there is also time for them to place realistic demands upon themselves professionally and also to let go. A good work–life balance is needed to help staff recuperate and settings need to

> *find ways to make it safe for staff and leaders (as well as pupils) to acknowledge their human distress, weakness and difficulty and seek support and help for their mental health needs in non-stigmatised ways.*
>
> (Weare, 2015, p7)

At a simple level, schools, teachers and leaders, by expressing gratitude and appreciation for the role that individuals can play in helping promote positive self-esteem within its pupils can be a quick but effective way of building a teacher's self-esteem. Try and make a habit of telling your teacher colleagues how much they are appreciated since well-being must start with the staff as they are at the chalkface of any work with regard to promoting pupils self-esteem.

- Remember if you are trying to support self-esteem there are no quick fixes.

- Encourage staff to be realistic of what can be achieved and that this success will ebb and flow given that some of the good work achieved in schools can be quickly undone by risk factors at home.

- Consider that self-esteem is like a non-stick surface; most of what is tried will slide off.

- Small incremental gains can be made, so encourage your staff not to lose heart or patience.

- Make certain that there is always an open door so that teachers can share worries, concerns and disillusionment with regard to progress.

- Be there to reassure them that they are doing a good job and that any perceived failure is not down to them.

 KEY REFLECTIONS

- What strategies can a school employ to improve resilience and the self-esteem of its pupils?
- What strategies might parents be told to use to support issues around self-esteem?
- What can colleagues do to support positive self-esteem amongst themselves?

CHAPTER SUMMARY

- Self-esteem is about how one thinks about oneself in relation to others.
- Self-esteem is sensitive to the qualities of these systems such as families, schools and communities and thus can be negative or positive.
- Relationships are at the heart of well-being and self-esteem.
- Positive self-esteem is aligned with happiness.
- Low self-esteem is aligned with unhappiness.
- Positive self-esteem includes protective characteristics or 'resilience' factors including a positive image of oneself, making friends easily, being able to solve problems and ask for help if needed, admitting mistakes and being able to adapt to change.
- Resilience factors can be influenced and improved through positive promotion of resilience in schools.
- Schools have opportunities to offer targeted support for at risk groups and can play a key role in improving resilience factors and thus self-esteem.
- Educational resilience is not just about academic performance but it includes development of relationships and social skills.

FURTHER READING

Hunter, C. (2012) *Is resilience still a useful concept when working with children and young people?* Child, Family, Community, Australia. Available at: https://aifs.gov.au/cfca/publications/resilience-still-useful-concept-when-working-child/export.

REFERENCES

Bandura, A. (1977) *Social Learning Theory.* Englewood Cliffs, NJ: Prentice Hall.

Bandura, A. (1989) Human agency in social cognitive theory. *American Psychologist*, 44(9): 1175–1184.

Bono, J.E. and Judge, T.A. (2003) Core self-evaluations: A review of the trait and its role in job satisfaction and job performance. *European Journal of Personality*, 17: S5–S18.

Burton, M., Pavord, E. and Williams, B. (2014) *An Introduction to Child and Adolescent Mental Health.* London: SAGE.

Children's Workforce Development Council (2009) *Early identification, assessment of needs and intervention: The Common Assessment Framework – A guide for practitioners.* Available at: http://webarchive. nationalarchives.gov.uk/20130401151715/https://www.education.gov.uk/publications/eordering download/caf-practitioner-guide.pdf (accessed March 2017).

Coleman, F. and Hagell, A. (2007) *Mental Health and Mental Disorders: Adolescence Risk and Resilience Against the Odds.* Chichester: John Wiley.

Department for Education (DfE) (2014) *Promoting the education of looked after children*. Available at: www.gov.uk/government/uploads/system/uploads/attachment_data/file/335964/Promoting_the_educational_achievement_of_looked_after_children_Final_23-....pdf (accessed January 2016).

Department for Education (2015) *Mental health and behaviour in schools*. Available at: www.gov.uk/government/uploads/system/uploads/attachment_data/file/416786/Mental_Health_and_Behaviour_-_Information_and_Tools_for_Schools_240515.pdf (accessed January 2016).

DfES (2005a) *Social and emotional aspects of learning (SEAL): Improving behaviour, improving learning*. Available at: http://webarchive.nationalarchives.gov.uk/20110809101133/nsonline.org.uk/node/87009 (accessed January 2016).

DfES (2005b) *Excellence and enjoyment: Social and emotional aspects of learning*. Norwich: HMSO. Available at: http://webarchive.nationalarchives.gov.uk/20110809101133/nsonline.org.uk/node/87009 (accessed January 2016).

Department of Health (DoH) (2011) *No health without mental health: A cross government mental health outcomes strategy for people of all ages*. Available at: www.gov.uk/government/uploads/system/uploads/attachment_data/file/213761/dh_124058.pdf (accessed January 2016).

Fuller, A. (1998) *From Surviving to Thriving: Promoting Mental Health in Young People*. Camberwell: The Australian Council for Educational Research Ltd.

Goleman, D. (1996) *Emotional Intelligence: Why It Can Matter More Than IQ*. London: Bloomsbury.

Joslyn, E. (2016) *Resilience in Children: Perspectives, Promise and Practice*. London: Palgrave.

Luxmoore, N. (2008) *Feeling like Crap: Young People and the Meaning of Self-esteem*. London: Jessica Kingsley.

Mental Health Foundation (2002) *A Bright Future for All: Promoting Mental Health in Education*. London: MHF.

Mosley, J. (2001) *Quality Circle Time in the Primary Classroom. Vol 1*. Cambridge: LDA.

Mosley, J. (2004) *More Quality Circle Time: Evaluating Your Practice and Developing Creativity Within the Whole School Quality Circle Time Model*. Cambridge: LDA.

Music, G. (2011) *Nurturing Natures: Attachment and Children's Sociocultural and Brain Development*. Hove, East Sussex: Psychology Press.

Newman, T. (2004) as cited in Coleman, F. and Hagell, A. (2007) *Mental Health and Mental Disorders, Adolescence Risk and Resilience Against the Odds*. Chichester: John Wiley, 14.

NSPCC (2015) 'Always there when I need you': ChildLine review: what's affecting children in April 2014–March 2015. London: NSPCC. Available at: www.nspcc.org.uk/services-and-resources/research-and-resources/2015/childline-annual-review-2014-2015-always-there/ (accessed January 2016).

Pearce, J. (1993) as cited in HAS Report (1995) *'Together We Stand': The Commissioning, Role and Management of CAMHS*. London: HMSO, 23.

Plummer, D. and Harper, A. (2007) *Helping Children to Build Self-Esteem: A Photocopiable Activities Book*. London: Jessica Kingsley.

Rees, G., Andresen, S. and Bradshaw, J.R. (eds) (2016) *Children's Views on Their Lives and Well-being in 16 Countries: A report on the Children's Worlds Survey of Children Aged Eight Years Old: 2013–15*. Zurich: Jacobs Foundation.

Rutter, M. (1985) Resilience in the face of adversity: Protective factors and resistance to psychiatric disorders. *British Journal of Psychiatry,* 147: 589–611.

Rutter, M. (1987) as cited in Werner, E. and Smith, R. (2001) *Journeys from Childhood to Midlife: Risk, Resilience and Recovery*. New York: Cornell, 3.

Rutter, M. (2006) Implications of resilience concepts for scientific understanding. *Annals of the New York Academy of Science,* 1094: 1–12.

Rutter, M. (2012) Resilience as a dynamic concept. *Development and Psychopathology,* 24: 335–344.

Scholfield, G., Ward, E., Biggart, L., Scaife, V., Dodsworth, J., Larsson, B., Haynes, A. and Stone, N. (2012) *Looked after children and offending*. Centre for Research on the Child and Family, University of East Anglia. Available at: www.tactcare.org.uk/data/files/resources/52/lac_and_offending_reducing_risk_promoting_resilience_fullreport_200212.pdf (accessed January 2016).

The Children's Society (2015) *The good childhood report 2015*. Available at: www.childrenssociety.org.uk/sites/default/files/TheGoodChildhoodReport2015.pdf (accessed January 2016).

UNICEF (2007) *Report Card 7: 'An overview of child well-being in rich countries'*. Available at: www.unicef-irc.org/publications/pdf/rc7_eng.pdf (accessed January 2016).

UNICEF (2011) *Report Card 11: 'An overview of child well-being in rich countries'*. Available at: www.unicef.org.uk/Images/Campaigns/FINAL_RC11-ENG-LORES-fnl2.pdf (accessed January 2016).

Weare, K. (2015) *What Works in Promoting Social and Emotional Well-being and Responding to Mental Health Problems in School?* London: National Children's Bureau.

Werner, E. and Smith, R.S. (2001) *Journeys from Childhood to Midlife: Risk, Resilience and Recovery*. New York: Cornell University Press.

Williams, N. (2016) *State of children's rights in England 2016: Briefing Paper 4 – Safeguarding*. Children's Rights Alliance England (CRAE). Available at: www.crae.org.uk/media/118308/crae_scr2016_b4_safeguarding-web.pdf (accessed March 2017).

Young Minds (2016) *About self-esteem*. Available at: www.youngminds.org.uk/for_parents/whats_worrying_you_about_your_child/self-esteem/about_self-esteem (accessed January 2016).

5

BULLYING, SOCIAL MEDIA AND PROMOTING RESILIENCE

Chapter objectives

By the end of this chapter you should be aware of:

- the importance of establishing a positive culture to enhance mental health and well-being;
- the need to have a zero tolerance towards bullying;
- the impact of bullying and the influence of social media on children and young people's well-being;
- what effective personal, social and health education (PSHE) looks like in the classroom;
- using PSHE to promote positive body image in classrooms;
- how to promote resilience in learning contexts relating to bullying, social media and body image through a whole school approach;
- how to use a creative curriculum to develop self-efficacy and emotional resilience in children.

Teachers' Standards

This chapter supports the development of the following Teachers' Standards:

TS1: Set high expectations which inspire, motivate and challenge pupils

- Establish a safe and stimulating environment for pupils, rooted in mutual respect.

TS5: Adapt teaching to respond to the strengths and needs of all pupils

- Demonstrate an awareness of the physical, social and intellectual development of children, and know how to adapt teaching to support pupils' education at different stages of development.

TS7: Manage behaviour effectively to ensure a good and safe learning environment

- Have clear rules and routines for behaviour in classrooms, and take responsibility for promoting good and courteous behaviour both in classrooms and around the school, in accordance with the school's behaviour policy.
- Have high expectations for behaviour, and establish a framework for discipline with a range of strategies, using praise, sanctions and rewards consistently and fairly.

TS8: Fulfil wider professional responsibilities

- Make a positive contribution to the wider life and ethos of the school.
- Communicate effectively with parents with regard to pupils' achievements and well-being.

Part Two: Personal and Professional Conduct

- Having regard for the need to safeguard pupils' well-being, in accordance with statutory provisions.

Introduction

The chapter will consider the impact of external factors on a child/young person's mental health and well-being, specifically looking at the impact of bullying, both in a real world context and also the growing concerns of the virtual world. The chapter will also examine the issues and challenges around children and young people's use of social media and how body image can influence individuals' feelings towards a sense of positive well-being. The role of the school will be considered and strategies and approaches which promote the building of resilience to all these pressures through the promotion of a whole school values system will be highlighted. Links will also be made to the role of the parents and carers in the positive use of social media sites and the use of phones and tablets.

Bullying

> *Bullying is the repetitive, intentional hurting of one person or group by another person or group, where the relationship involves an imbalance of power. Bullying can be physical, verbal or psychological. It can happen face-to-face or in cyberspace.*

(Children's Commissioner, 2017a)

It is vital that children and young people have the right to come to school and to be able to focus on their studies, free from disruption and the fear of bullying. This will not only help them flourish academically but socially too. Schools and the police have powers to stop bullying taking place and have a responsibility to ensure children and young people are safe. The Good Childhood Report (Children's Society, 2016) gives us an indication of the scale of bullying and how it affects children, young people, parents and carers, as well as teachers in school. From just under 6,000 respondents, it became clear that a bullying culture can have a significant impact on the mental health and well-being of children and young people. Of those surveyed:

- 42 per cent had to take time off school because of bullying.

- 67 per cent felt depressed as a result of bullying.

- 90 per cent of the bullying took place at school.

- 57 per cent were bullied on Facebook.

- 38 per cent were bullied on Instagram.

- 32 per cent were bullied on Snapchat.

- 50 per cent of young people were bullied about their appearance.

Despite an overall decrease in bullying in schools, there still remain groups of children who are more likely to be bullied than others, including those living in extreme poverty, disabled children, children from black and minority ethnic communities and LGBTQ children and young people. A recent survey of young people found that 45 per cent who had been bullied in the past year did not feel that their school or college took bullying seriously. 21 per cent thought that teachers needed more anti-bullying training and 19 per cent wanted more lessons and activities designed to combat bullying. Reports of an increase in racist language by students in schools after the EU Referendum are also concerning. On a positive note, the government has invested in eight projects to prevent and tackle homophobic, biphobic and transphobic bullying in schools by improving school policies and training. It has also made a commitment to carry out an assessment of the level of anti-Muslim, anti-Semitic, homophobic, racist and other bullying in schools to inform further action to reduce levels of such bullying. In addition, there is a commitment to assess the amount of anti-Muslim, anti-Semitic and homophobic bullying in order to inform appropriate action (Children's Rights Alliance for England, 2016a, p8). There was a recommendation that the government should take urgent action to address discrimination experienced by many groups of children, especially in relation to bullying and school exclusions. Serious concerns have also been raised about aspects of the 'Prevent' strategy and its impact on education. There is now a statutory duty on teachers and many public servants to report signs of radicalisation, and it has been noted that this is stifling fundamental rights and freedoms of children, including freedom of expression and belief. It has been demonstrated that Muslim children have been disproportionately impacted and fear being reported for expressing political and religious views. The National Union of Teachers passed a motion rejecting the Prevent strategy in 2016 (Children's Rights Alliance for England, 2016b).

The Royal College of Psychiatrists (2017) suggests bullying can have a direct impact on mental health and well-being leading to depression, feelings of loneliness and a lack of confidence in individuals. Given all of this concerning evidence of the negative effect bullying has on individuals, it would seem vital that all schools have robust systems for identifying and dealing with bullying. Sadly, in cases of self-harm and completed suicides amongst children and young people, bullying is frequently cited as a trigger or a reason and is often a significant contributing factor, as discussed in Chapter 1. Each setting should have a zero acceptance policy of any such type of bullying if we are to help our children and young people deal with such a serious issue.

With the release of the DfE (2010) White Paper *The Importance of Teaching*, the government also made it clear that poor discipline is responsible for decreased levels of retention within the teaching workforce. The lack of respect towards teaching staff in general and the impact it has on their health and well-being has been linked to staff leaving the profession, with good teachers being forced out of the classroom. The White Paper contained a number of key recommendations to ensure schools create a

> *culture of respect and safety, with zero tolerance of bullying, clear boundaries, good pastoral care and early intervention to address problems.*

> (DfE, 2010, p32)

The revised Ofsted School Inspection Handbook (2015a) incorporated these key recommendations into its framework, with a greater focus on behaviour and safety as one of the core areas for schools' consideration, linked to the well-being and health of individuals when in school. The framework now includes monitoring whether children feel safe in school and are protected from bullying in the playground, corridors and also in the classroom. Record-keeping of bullying incidents will be monitored as well as, more importantly, how the school has responded to these incidences to ensure a zero tolerance approach. Evidence will also be reviewed from parents and carers. The grade descriptors for a school to obtain 'Outstanding' for personal development, behaviour and welfare include requirements that schools ensure that:

- Pupils work hard with the school to prevent all forms of bullying, including online bullying and prejudice-based bullying.

- Staff and pupils deal effectively with the very rare instances of bullying behaviour and/or use of derogatory or aggressive language.

- The school's open culture actively promotes all aspects of pupils' welfare. Pupils are safe and feel safe at all times. They understand how to keep themselves and others safe in different situations and settings. They trust leaders to take rapid and appropriate action to resolve any concerns they have.

- Pupils can explain accurately and confidently how to keep themselves healthy. They make informed choices about healthy eating, fitness and their emotional and mental well-being. They have an age-appropriate understanding of healthy relationships and are confident in staying safe from abuse and exploitation.

- Pupils have an excellent understanding of how to stay safe online and of the dangers of inappropriate use of mobile technology and social networking sites (Ofsted, 2015a, p51).

In 2012, Ofsted produced a document entitled *No Place for Bullying*, to give schools guidance on how to create a positive culture and prevent and tackle bullying. The document outlined a national survey which looked at how effective schools were in tackling bullying through a whole school approach. Key to ensuring a positive culture was an embedded high quality behaviour policy which was consistently and regularly used by staff and children, training for teachers and support staff in order to build expertise, knowledge and confidence in using inclusive language and also how to effectively deal with negative behaviours and most importantly, a clear vision shared by all in the school, with clear values permeating through the curriculum and school environment. Not only should a behaviour policy underpin such a positive school culture for dealing with and preventing bullying and the effects it has on mental health and well-being, it should be remembered that such a policy is a statutory requirement for all schools (DfE, 2012).

Research by Yeager and Dweck (2012) has shown the importance of resilience for success in school life and in particular the role that an individual's mindset can play in their resilience to social challenges such as being bullied. They suggest that promoting a move from a fixed view of a person's characteristics or ability (fixed or entity theory) to that of a more developmental view of how abilities or characteristics grow and develop (incremental theory) may allow for individuals to see a brighter future for themselves as well as a desire to understand the motives of the transgressor. Although, given this, it is important that professionals should never seek to minimise the seriousness and impact of the bullying on the victim by the perpetrator and should also never seek to ascribe a sense of responsibility on the victim for the situation they unfortunately find themselves in. It is important to note that such research has shown that mindsets can be changed and that such differences can lead to the promotion of resilience. As Yeager and Dweck (2012, p310) note:

when adolescents have or are taught a mindset in which people have potential to change their socially relevant traits – even if those traits are difficult to change – then they can be more resilient in the face of victimization or exclusion.

Through their use of PSHE strategies such as socially speaking and circle time, schools can support children's views of how bullying should be perceived by the victim and perpetrator and dealt with. Strategies such as restorative justice can be used in schools to help victims and bullies come together to seek a shared understanding of the impact of bullying on all those involved and to see if common ground and a new perspective can be found.

Cyberbullying

Though in the past bullying may have been confined mainly to the school setting, it has nowadays evolved to include technology as a means to facilitate 'virtual' bullying or cyberbullying (DfE, 2014b). Currently, statistical data relating to cyberbullying is limited; behaviour statistics published by the Department of Education (reported by Adams, 2015), however, indicate that 11 per cent of children had experienced cyberbullying, with girls appearing to be more at risk from cyberbullying than boys. 15 per cent of girls indicated that they had encountered such a form of bullying whilst only 7 per cent of boys indicated this. Smith et al. (2006) agree that girls are significantly more likely to be cyberbullied than boys but add that girls are more likely to ask for help than boys. Li (2006) explains that this may be due to differences in conversational styles and gender roles in society; males tend to not ask for help or discuss problems, viewing it as a sign of weakness, whereas girls are not likely to take this into consideration.

Currently there is an upward trend in internet usage amongst children and young people; this correlates with the increasing concern regarding the dangers of the internet (Ofcom, 2013; Subrahmanyam and Greenfield, 2008). These dangers are particularly related to exposure to inappropriate content, cyberbullying and making harmful contacts online (Valkenburg and Peter, 2010). Research also demonstrates that there is a need to balance the opportunities of the internet with the dangers and also to educate parents/carers regarding the positive aspects of the internet, rather than purely sensationalise the dangers (Tynes, 2007).

Given the recent rise in ownership of mobile devices by children, and their involvement in aspects of social media, it seems inevitable that statistics such as those detailed earlier are unlikely as yet to improve. As the DfE (2014b, p6) suggests:

cyber-bullying is a different form of bullying and can happen at all times of the day, with a potentially bigger audience, and more accessories as people forward on content at a click.

Sharples et al. (2009) suggest that children are well aware of internet dangers such as cyberbullying but are not trusted to self-regulate their behaviour. Parents are out of date and unable to impose appropriate safeguards, and schools are balancing the use of the internet for creativity, community and personal learning with their pupils' safety. Therefore children/young people's online activity becomes a tool for attributing blame and can be viewed with a sense of unease and distrust by adults, leaving children/young people to negotiate this themselves (Duerager and Livingstone, 2012).

With these perspectives in mind, children/young people can either be seen as vulnerable, with the internet posing a risk to their cognitive and social development, or as competent and creative, IT-literate and in need of a rich, stimulating online environment. Livingstone (2009) argues that it is these historical changes to childhood that reposition children in society and can even impede their passage to adulthood.

> *Excessive use of social media when combined with bullying has been linked to poor mental health problems. Felix Alexander was a 17-year-old who took his life after years of relentless bullying. Social media takes away the boundaries that school, social groups or communities used to provide. Online bullying that no longer stops at the end of the school day can seem relentless and 24/7 in nature when it happens.*

> (Children's Commissioner, 2016b)

For schools, professionals and children and young people, cyberbullying can be found to be linked to threats and intimidation, harassment, unwanted peer pressure and unauthorised access to accounts. As Childnet International (2016) suggests, a disproportionate number of individuals with special education needs and disabilities, and learners identifying as gay, lesbian, bisexual or transgender, are affected by cyberbullying.

For schools, cyberbullying can be at the root of causing issues allied to children and young people's feelings of positive self-worth and well-being, and can also be linked to safeguarding issues such as downloading inappropriate web content and sexting (sending an individual explicit images or messages via a mobile device). Research demonstrates that children and young people's attitudes to sexting varies, from those who do not see it as a major issue to those who deem it potentially damaging or illegal (Lenhart, 2009). The issue is not helped by unclear terminology, exaggerated findings and less emphasis on reasons for sexting (Lounsbury et al., 2012).

Cyberbullying content and activities may actually be illegal given they may involve the inclusion and distribution of indecent materials. Such illegal usage may fall under the Communications Act 2003, Section 127, where it is considered a crime to send an electronic message which is of a grossly offensive nature or is indecent, obscene or even of a menacing character (NSPCC, 2017). Should any school believe that the content or activity linked to the internet in schools is illegal, then they should contact the police for help and support as soon as is possible, as well as following any suitable safeguarding practices. The Professionals Online Safety Helpline can provide schools with free advice and guidance relating to any cyberbullying concerns. Importantly, schools should remember that they also have powers under the Education Act 2011 for teaching professionals to tackle cyberbullying by providing them with the authority to search for inappropriate content on electronic devices. There are additional resources for these issues in the further reading section of this chapter.

Childnet International (2016, p12) suggests that in order to start dealing with such issues, schools should consider the following proactive measures:

- promote a shared understanding and awareness about cyberbullying;

- keep policies up to date and current;

- make reporting easier so as to stop the incident from escalating and to remove the items from circulation;

- promote the positive uses of technology;

- work with key safeguarding authorities such as the police and the local authority to gain support in terms of guidance and training;

- in England, use the Computing Programmes of Study for primary and secondary schools to promote internet safety;

- use the citizenship curriculum, PSHE, as well as religious education (RE);

- make individuals aware of school sanctions that may follow if cyberbullying is found to be present in such settings;

- involve parents so that they too can support the promotion to eradicate such behaviours.

Research by Phippen (2016) identified, when examining online policy and practice, that almost 60 per cent of schools had no engagement regarding online safety issues with regard to their community and that 55 per cent of school governors had not been trained in online safety issues. Clearly, schools should work to involve other stakeholders so that they too can help educate children and young people as well as promote online safety for the children and young people in their care. In order to make the right decisions, children and young people need to feel empowered with the correct knowledge and confidence to act accordingly. Katz (2012) suggests that internet safety educators should build on the child/young person's self-efficacy and autonomy and find out what they know in order to be successful.

In relation to supporting parents/carers in keeping their child safe online, research demonstrates that children and young people who talked about internet safety with their parents were more knowledgeable and confident regarding appropriate action (Fleming et al., 2006). Therefore parents/carers should be encouraged to talk with their child about the internet and their usage and promote the positives whilst being mindful and vigilant of the dangers.

The South West Grid for Learning has produced free to access support materials, along with curricular guidance, linked to supporting and improving digital literacy. This encourages individuals to think critically, as well as to promote safe, responsible participation in our digital world. The materials may be found at **www.digital-literacy.org.uk/Curriculum-Overviewaspx**. Such material may also support schools' work in their computing curriculum which will no doubt aim to provide online safety education as part of its delivery. Further information regarding online safety linked to the computing curriculum may be found at **www.childnet.com/resources/esafety-and-computing**.

KEY REFLECTIONS

- How can bullying affect mental health and well-being?
- What is cyberbullying?
- What strategies and powers can schools use to support children who have encountered cyberbullying?

Establishing the culture and communicating expectations

Evidence from the National Children's Bureau (Stirling and Emery, 2016) *A Whole School Framework for Emotional Well-Being and Mental Health* reinforces the importance of a whole school approach in order to embed a culture of acceptance and respect for children and young people. The senior management team in a school are responsible for ensuring that shared values are made clear to all stakeholders, including children, young people, staff, parents, governors and the wider community, and that all buy into ensuring that these are manifested in the life of the school. This may be achieved by establishing a clear vision for what the school stands for. By doing so it will ensure that children and young people feel part of a safe community and that they understand what is acceptable and not acceptable behaviour with such expectations being continually reinforced by staff. Clear school policies for behaviour linked to bullying should be consistently embedded across the whole school and shared with parents on the school website.

As part of the United Nations Convention on the Rights to the Child (UNCRC) Article 12 (UNICEF 1992) and as part of good practice, schools should also ensure that the pupil's voice is valued as part of the policy through school councils so that issues can be aired in a supportive way. This ensures that children and young people are active participants in their own educational experience. Pupils who are vulnerable should be identified and a clear strategy for support highlighted and embedded in the SEND policy. Research shown in the DfE (2016) document *Mental Health and Behaviour in Schools* clearly identifies factors which put children and young people at greater risk of mental health issues, and one of these factors is low self-esteem. In a school environment this could be due to bullying, discrimination, peer pressure or breakdown in friendship groups. Protective factors that schools could put in place are clear behaviour and bullying policies as well as a whole school approach to promoting positive mental health and well-being, as discussed in Chapter 2.

 **KEY REFLECTIONS**

- How is your school's vision being effectively translated into meaningful learning experiences for all the pupils and what factors impact on these in your school?
- How up to date and relevant are your policies given the changing face of bullying?

Impact of social media: body image

Due to the increased pressures of social media, the prevalence of the printed image and their access to film and television, children and young people can now more easily access imagery and messages that not only reflect the way they 'should' look but also how they 'should' behave in order to satisfy the norms of what society portrays as being socially acceptable.

Major findings from the report *Somebody Like Me* (BEREAL, 2017, pp4–5) worryingly indicate that:

- Four in five young people (79 per cent) said how they look is important to them.

- Nearly two-thirds of young people (63 per cent) said what others think about the way they look is important to them.

- More than half of young people (52 per cent) said they often worry about the way they look.

- More than a third of young people (36 per cent) agreed they would do whatever it took to look good.

- Almost three in five young people (57 per cent) have, or would consider, going on a diet to change the way they look.

- One in ten young people (10 per cent) said they would consider plastic surgery to change the way they look.

It is also important not to assume that body image issues linked to an individual's well-being and mental health will be centred on girls alone. As the PSHE Association (2017, p7) suggests:

- over half of girls and a quarter of boys think their peers have body image problems;

- one third of young boys aged 8–12 are dieting to lose weight.

The Good Childhood Report (2016) also provides an overview of variations and trends through an eight-year longitudinal study linked to the state of children's subjective well-being. One of the aspects researched is the gender differences in satisfaction with appearance. A key finding was that since 2002, there has been a long term trend of divergence in satisfaction with appearance for boys and girls, with girls becoming increasingly unhappy with their appearance, friends and marginally with life as a whole. Children were asked to talk about their feelings and a main theme that the research found was that how they looked was an important factor in determining their well-being.

With the proliferation of the use of social media such as Instagram, Snapchat, selfies and the growth of vloggers, girls in particular have access to images and videos presenting the rise of unattainable 'perfection' – how to have the perfect body, lifestyle, friends, clothes, make up and beauty products.

Subscriptions to some of these vloggers on YouTube are increasing rapidly, with popular vloggers like 'Zoella' having over 11 million followers. Linked to the influence that celebrities like Zoe Sugg (Zoella) have with young girls, MindEd unveiled her as one of their digital ambassadors in 2014 due to her videos talking about her own struggles with anxiety and panic attacks.

The attempt to dispel the myth of perfection is a positive way forward, allowing an opportunity for children and young people, particularly girls, to see that everyone has insecurities and problems in their lives; the important thing is that it is crucial to talk about them. However, as teachers, it is important to note when considering issues around body confidence that your use of language is crucial, and you should avoid commenting on changes to an individual's body, behaviour and appearance, even if such comments are of a positive nature. It is important that individuals are happy with their own personal qualities rather than constantly considering how others view them. As the National Advisory Group (2009, p43) suggests:

> *Teachers are important models for students and their language about their own body image or comments about others can inadvertently communicate negative body image messages to students.*

(2009, p43)

PSHE as a curriculum vehicle

School settings can play a significant role in supporting children and young people in the growth of improved body confidence and self-esteem as part of their current PSHE curriculum. This can be allied to aspects of schools' work on healthy lifestyles and the need to engage in physical activities.

The Ten Principles of PSHE Education (available at **www.pshe-association.org.uk**) show that good practice applied to any work relating to issues around body image should include:

- Planning of a 'spiral programme' which introduces new and more challenging learning, while building on what has gone before, which reflects and meets the personal developmental needs of the children and young people.

- Start from where the children and young people are … For maximum impact involve them in the planning of your PSHE programme.

- Take a positive approach which does not attempt to induce shock or guilt.

- Provide opportunities for children and young people to make real decisions about their lives.

- Provide a safe and supportive learning environment where children and young people can develop the confidence to ask questions, challenge the information they are offered, draw on their own experience, express their views and opinions and put what they have learnt into practice in their own lives.

As previously mentioned in this chapter, the values embedded throughout the school are vital for children to feel safe and happy. A culture of openness in the classroom, where children feel comfortable to talk about their feelings and worries, is the duty of the whole school. The language that we use in front of children needs careful consideration to ensure we are acting as positive role models and not reinforcing negative and unrealistic perceptions. Conversations that can easily occur in the classroom or corridors amongst adults about dieting, comments about particular parts of body – 'fat shaming' – or talking about celebrities in the press can send mixed messages to children if we are working towards a positive body image programme in the school.

Consider the following case study and begin to establish ideas for practice and strategies your school might use to support the issue of positive body image.

CASE STUDY: PROMOTING POSITIVE BODY IMAGE

Ofsted (2015b) have produced an excellent case study of how a school had promoted good practice regarding their positive body image programme through the teaching of PSHE across the whole school. The project began with training for staff and parents to highlight the impact of social media on perceptions of body image on children. From this a programme of work was developed with the option of additional staff training, if needed, linked to specific topics. Part of the programme included the Dove campaign which linked to peer pressure and unrealistic ideas around body image. The school programme was designed to include children from Year 1 up to Year 6 using PSHE as a vehicle to teach a spiral curriculum based on age related needs of the children. In Key Stage 1, children were encouraged to think about similarities and differences between themselves and others and to start to encourage positive self-esteem and appreciation of difference. In Key Stage 2 children began to look at the impact of the media and the influence this had on them. Topics such as celebrity culture, digital enhancement, cosmetic surgery, genetics and also the different cultural definitions of beauty were developed. Children were encouraged to talk about their own experiences, expressing their own views and opinions in a safe learning environment. Work was encouraged to be shared with parents and carers at home to enable parents to be able to confidently talk about some of these issues with their children. Feedback from the children, staff and parents about this programme was extremely positive and children felt empowered to accept their own bodies and confident to challenge any negativity or stereotypical language.

Case study reflections

- What training has your staff had around body image?
- Does promoting issues around body image feature in your PSHE curriculum?
- How does your school communicate with parents around issues to do with body image?

The PSHE Association strongly recommends that when talking about body image in your classrooms this should dovetail with teaching around healthy eating and lifestyle in order for children to associate both together as a lifestyle choice. The PSHE Association (2015) has produced detailed guidance in terms of their Key Standards in Teaching about Body Image with this guidance linking to programmes of study around the themes of 'health and well-being', 'relationships' and 'living in the wider world' in Key Stages 1–4 (**www.pshe-association.org.uk/curriculum-and-resources/resources/key-standards-teaching-about-body-image**). The importance of the pupil voice and the personalisation of the teaching content are crucial to the success of the programme – helping children to talk about things that are important to them without fear of bullying or embarrassment is a skill that teachers need to master. This links to the Ofsted case study above where the first part of the programme was an intensive staff training session to ensure all adults were confident and equipped for the teaching programme. Knowing your class will inform your decisions about content, but there are also other factors to consider such as whether to teach single or mixed gender sessions and also whether there are children in your class who you know are affected by some of the issues being discussed. Ground rules about behaviour and a regular reinforcement of class and school values as discussed earlier in the chapter will be crucial at this point to establish a safe and respectful environment.

Teachers have a duty to safeguard children, and one of the biggest concerns is around disclosure. Creating an open and honest environment needs to be balanced by clear rules which ensure children and young people understand that we do not discuss our own personal or private lives in the session, use names or put any peers or teachers on the spot. All children have the right to decide not to participate if they do not feel comfortable. Teachers cannot promise that information would not be shared if we felt a child was at risk of harm. Teachers should ensure they follow the school safeguarding policy.

As well as promoting this topic through the vehicle of PSHE there are various other ways in which children and young people can provide input into the content of the teaching programme. These include for example the use of worry boxes either in classrooms, corridors or in toilets, use of the school council or pupil leadership team and the use of Clickers using interactive whiteboards and completion of anonymised questionnaires. Curriculum subjects can be used to promote reflection on aspects of body image and confidence such as science linked to evolution, inheritance and history, and how, through diet and lifestyle, our appearance and bodies have changed. In addition to this, much valuable advice and support for schools can be found from BEREAL who have produced an extremely useful toolkit for school to help support and tackle issues around body confidence. This can be found at **www.berealcampaign.co.uk/schools**.

CASE STUDY: 'PITMASTON POWERS' BUILDING RESILIENCE THROUGH THE CURRICULUM

In the document *Closing the Gap* (NCTL, 2014) with the New Primary National Curriculum (DfE, 2013), key barriers to learning were identified in relation to disadvantaged children receiving pupil premium money. The requirement to close gaps in attainment for these children is a high priority for schools and this report showcased work carried out by 12 teaching school alliances to share good practice of how they had implemented and embedded practice in their schools in line with the new National Curriculum. The findings of this report will serve to inspire schools to develop projects of their own through school improvement planning and also encourage teachers to start professional dialogue and also to identify training needs through continued professional development.

One of the case studies linked to building resilience was based on the work of Guy Claxton (2002) in Building Learning Power (BLP) through four domains of learning: resilience, reflectiveness, reciprocity and resourcefulness. These were introduced to the children through the establishment of 'superhero character puppets' and focused mainly on the domain of resilience. This was successful due to the way this approach was valued by all stakeholders and mirrored the clear vision and ethos of the school.

This case study has inspired a large primary school in Worcestershire to develop this approach in the school through the launch of 'Pitmaston Powers' across the whole school. Staff training around the theme of 'What makes a good learner at our school?' led to the identification of 'Powers' which

(Continued)

(Continued)

teachers would look for in children to enable them to become successful learners. This approach built on their current and recent strategies embedded within the school, such as Bloom's Taxonomy (Bloom et al., 1956), learning pits, achievement for all (**www.afaeducation.org**) and Thrive (**www.thriveapproach.com**) with the view that the 'Powers' would lead to further development of the curriculum, their understanding of greater depth in learning and the children's capacity to learn.

The concept of 'Pitmaston Powers' was introduced to all of the children across the school in the first week of the new academic year. The children were with a new teacher and in a new learning environment so establishing a safe community of learners to enable children to transition successfully was crucial. Therefore the discussion around what makes good learners was a timely and useful activity to complete at this point. Following the introduction, children themselves were encouraged to identify their own ideas around learning powers and all ideas were taken to the pupil leadership group where, with the pupil voice as the heart of this process, the final Powers were agreed. Following this process, the children then worked with teachers to create characters and heroes linked to each of the 'Powers'.

The 'Pitmaston Powers' were embedded throughout the school using learning heroes and characters with the challenge for children to use opportunities to build their 'learning muscles' and develop 'supple learning minds' through establishing enabling and supportive learning environments. The 'Powers' that were identified as 'Pitmaston Powers' are:

- Resilience
- Positivity
- Independence
- Motivation
- Reflection

Following the identification of the 'Powers', a staff training session was carried out to ensure that a shared understanding of what these powers looked like was clear and consistent across the whole school and a strategy on how they can be embedded into the curriculum was developed. It was key that all teachers were clear and confident that they understood the importance that the learning power muscles should be built on every day and clear links to children's mental health and well-being identified.

'Pitmaston Powers' was then launched by the pupil leadership team through whole school assemblies to enable them to be active participants in the project. Subsequent assemblies were carried out based on the ideas from Place2Be (**www.place2be.org.uk**) and launched with an assembly on resilience with the theme of 'get through difficult times and bounce forward'. These guides are suitable for all primary aged children with clear aims identified, resources needed and clear key teaching points outlined. The assemblies begin with sharing a personal story of a recent event in school in order to personalise the assembly and give it meaning to the children in the assembly. Extension activities are included in the guide so teachers can follow up on key themes back in the classroom and a time for reflection completes the assembly with suggested exit songs.

A whole school approach was facilitated through the production of posters and stickers linked to each of the 'Powers' and certificates available to celebrate learning powers. Parents were encouraged to get involved through newsletters and information provided on the school website.

Developing emotional resilience and self-efficacy using a creative curriculum approach

Self-efficacy can be defined as *the belief in one's capabilities to organise and execute behaviours required to produce given attainments* (Bandura, 1977, 1997). What is important to note is that self-efficacy is about the learners' perception and not the reality in being able to carry out a task. This belief in personal capability can therefore be linked to emotional resilience. This is easily dented, as discussed earlier, with regard to aspects of bullying and children and young people's feelings about themselves. If a child has self-belief that they can do something, even if they are unsuccessful initially, this can have positive implications on developing positive well-being in the classroom. A recent study carried out by Hewitt et al. (2017) on initial teacher primary education students linked to building understanding of self-efficacy and emotional resilience using a programme of dramatherapy (Jennings, 1992) workshops showed some interesting outcomes which have implications for practice in schools. First, self-efficacy on the part of the teacher shows a clear impact on pupil achievement, pupil motivation and pupil self-efficacy (Gonzales-DeHass and Willems, 2013). This links back clearly to the point made earlier in this chapter that staff training is crucial in order for knowledge and skills to be consistently understood and embedded across the school. A teacher also has to have the belief and confidence in being able to teach and model appropriate behaviours and content to the children in their care. The programme of dramatherapy used in the study could also have interesting links to the use of a creative curriculum approach in schools as it enables participants to express their feelings, such as anxiety, self-doubt and lack of self-belief, through problem-solving activities, with the outcome of developing coping strategies and skills which build resilience, particularly when faced with future challenges and new contexts. In the study, a dramatherapist was used to deliver creative and therapeutic workshops to the students as interventions focused on developing their resilience, self-efficacy and confidence through art, drama, dance and music activities in a safe and supportive environment. Seven workshops were embedded into the teaching programme at key points during an academic year; all of these were experiential and focused on key topics such as obstacles in education for children and teachers and the importance of resilience. Students were able to think about and explore their own feelings and also practise developing skills such as emotional resilience, coping skills and building relationships. The study showed clear improvements in resilience for the students who took part in the study and an effective intervention for use with student teachers.

KEY REFLECTIONS

- How does your school promote resilience in children and young people?
- What strategies do you currently have in place to support children and young people's well-being?
- How can the school curriculum be used to support aspects of individuals' resilience?

CHAPTER SUMMARY

- Bullying can have a lasting impact on children and young people's mental health and well-being.
- Schools should have a zero tolerance approach to bullying in whatever form.
- Cyberbullying is an increasingly worrying concern for schools and children and young people.
- Cyberbullying can lead to criminal acts as well as having a negative influence on children and young people's mental health and well-being.
- A whole school approach to bullying is needed, with clear expectations for individuals' behaviour.
- Social media and societal expectations are resulting in issues of mental health and well-being centred on body image.
- Schools need clear strategies to support individuals with the teaching and understanding of issues centred around body image.

FURTHER READING

Anti-Bully Alliance (2014) *Bullying at school*. Available at: www.anti-bullyingalliance.org.uk/media/7468/bullying-and-the-law-may-14.pdf (accessed 12 January 2017).

Department for Education (2016) *Keeping Children Safe in Education: Statutory Guidance for Schools and Colleges*. London: Department of Education.

Government Equalities Office (2014) *Body confidence: Findings from the British Social Attitude Survey – October 2014*. Available at: www.gov.uk/government/publications/body-confidence-a-rapid-evidence-assessment-of-the-literature (accessed 5 February 2017).

Gov.UK (2016) *Bullying at school*. Available at: www.gov.uk/bullying-at-school/bullying-outside-school (accessed 12 January 2017).

NSPCC anti-bullying advice can be found at: www.nspcc.org.uk/preventing-abuse/child-abuse-and-neglect/online-abuse/legislation-policy-practice/.

Safer Internet can be found at: www.saferinternet.org.uk/about/helpline.

REFERENCES

Adams, R. (2015) 'Fewer school bullies but cyberbullying on the increase'. *The Guardian*. Available at: https://theguardian.com/society/2015/nov/16/bullying-at-school-in-decline-but-cyberbullying-is-on-the-increase (accessed 4 February 2017).

Bandura, A. (1977) Self-efficacy: Towards a unifying theory of behavioural change. *Psychology Review*, 84(2): 191–215.

Bandura, A. (1997) *Self-efficacy: The Exercise of Control*. New York: W.H. Freeman and Company.

BEREAL (2017) *Somebody like me: A report investigating the impact of body image anxiety on young people in the UK*. Available at: www.berealcampaign.co.uk/somebody-like-me (accessed 5 February 2017).

Bloom, B.S. (ed.), Engelhart, M.D., Furst, E.J., Hill, W.H. and Krathwohl, D.R. (1956) *Taxonomy of Educational Objectives: The Classification of Educational Goals. Handbook 1: Cognitive Domain*. New York: David McKay.

Childnet International (2016) *Cyberbullying: Understand, prevent and respond – Guidance for schools*. Available at: www.childnet.com/ufiles/Cyberbullying-guidance2.pdf (accessed 5 February 2017).

Children's Commissioner (2016a) *What is bullying?* Available at: www.childrenscommissioner.gov.uk/get-advice/questions/what-bullying (accessed 1 February 2017).

Children's Commissioner (2016b) *Children with mental health problems need help to recover and thrive*. Available at: www.childrenscommissioner.gov.uk/news/children-mental-health-problems-need-help-recover-and-thrive (accessed 1 February 2017).

Children's Rights Alliance for England (2016a) *State of Children's Rights in England 2016: Briefing 6 – Education, Leisure and Cultural Activities*. Available at: www.crae.org.uk/media/118310/crae_scr2016_b6_education-web.pdf (accessed 1 February 2017).

Children's Rights Alliance for England (2016b) *State of Children's Rights in England 2016: Briefing 2 – Children at the Centre, The General Measures and the General Principles of the CRC*. Available at: www.crae.org.uk/media/118306/crae_scr2016_b2_general-measures-web.pdf (accessed 1 February 2017).

The Children's Society (2016) *The Good Childhood Report 2016*. London: The Children's Society.

Claxton, G. (2002) *Building Learning Power: Helping Young People Become Better Learners*. Bristol: TLO Limited.

DfE (2010) *The importance of teaching: The schools white paper 2010*. Available at: www.gov.uk/government/uploads/system/uploads/attachment_data/file/175429/CM-7980.pdf (accessed 1 January 2017).

DfE (2012) *Ensuring good behaviour in schools: A summary for head teachers, governing bodies, teachers, parents and pupils*. Available at: http://dera.ioe.ac.uk/14113/1/Ensuring%20Good%20Behaviour%20in%20Schools%20-%20A%20summary%20for%20heads%20governing%20bodies%20teachers%20parents%20and%20pupils.pdf (accessed 7 February 2017).

DfE (2013) *National curriculum in England*. Available at: www.gov.uk/government/uploads/system/uploads/attachment_data/file/425601/PRIMARY_national_curriculum.pdf (accessed 15 January 2017).

DfE (2014a) *Mental health and behaviour in schools*. Available at: www.gov.uk/government/uploads/system/uploads/attachment_data/file/508847/Mental_Health_and_Behaviour_-_advice_for_Schools_160316.pdf (accessed 8 February 2017).

DfE (2014b) *Preventing and tackling bullying: Advice for head teachers, staff and governing bodies*. Available at: www.gov.uk/government/uploads/system/uploads/attachment_data/file/444862/Preventing_and_tackling_bullying_advice.pdf (accessed 6 February 2017).

DfE (2016) *Keeping children safe in education: Statutory guidance for schools and colleges*. Available at: www.gov.uk/government/publications/keeping-children-safe-in-education–2 (accessed 2 February 2017).

Duerager, A. and Livingstone, S. (2012) *How Can Parents Support Children's Internet Safety?* London: EU Kids Online.

Fleming, M., Greentree, S., Cocotti-Muller, D., Elias, K. and Morrison, S. (2006) Safety in cyberspace: Adolescents' safety and exposure online. *Youth & Society*, 38(2): 138–154.

Gonzales-DeHass, A.R. and Willems, P.P (2013) *Theories in Educational Psychology: Concise Guide to Meaning and Practice*. Plymouth: Rowman & Littlefield Education.

Hewitt, S., Buxton, S. and Thomas, A. (2017) A new way of learning: How can an understanding of self-efficacy and emotional resilience be used to develop successful teaching and learning strategies for students in initial teacher education. *Teacher Education Advancement Network Journal*, 9(1): 22–35.

Jennings, S. (1992) *Dramatherapy with Families, Groups and Individuals: Waiting in the Wings*. London: Jessica Kingsley Publications.

Katz, A. (2012) *Cyberbullying and E-Safety*. London: Jessica Kingsley Publishers.

Lenhart, A. (2009) Teens and Sexting. *Pew Internet & American Life Project*. Available at: www.pewinter net.org/files/old-media/Files/Reports/2009/PIP_Teens_and_Sexting.pdf (accessed 1 February 2017).

Li, Q. (2006) Cyberbullying in schools: A research of gender differences. *School Psychology International*, 27: 157–170.

Livingstone, S. (2009) *Children and the Internet: Great Expectations, Challenging Realities*. Cambridge: Polity Press.

Lounsbury, K., Mitchell, K. and Finkelhor, D. (2011) The true prevalence of 'Sexting'. *Crimes against Children Research Center*, 1–4. Available at: http://cola.unh.edu/sites/cola.unh.edu/files/research_pub lications/Sexting_Fact_Sheet_4_29_11.pdf (accessed 1 February 2017).

National Advisory Group (2009) *A proposed national strategy on body image*. Available at: www.eating disorderhope.com/pdf/Proposed-National-Strategy-on-Body-Image_australia.pdf (accessed 6 February 2017).

National Children's Bureau (2016) *A Whole School Framework for Emotional Well-being and Mental Health*. London: NCB.

NCTL (2014) *Closing the Gap with the New Primary National Curriculum*. Nottingham: NCTL. Ref: DFE-374. Available at: www.gov.uk/government/uploads/system/uploads/attachment_data/file/349288/closing-the-gap-with-the-new-primary-national-curriculum.pdf (accessed 28 January 2017).

NSPCC (2017) *Online abuse legislation, policy and practice*. Available at: www.nspcc.org.uk/preventing-abuse/child-abuse-and-neglect/online-abuse/legislation-policy-practice (accessed 7 January 2017).

Ofsted (2012) *No place for bullying: How schools create a positive culture and prevent and tackle bullying*. Ref: 110179. Available at: www.gov.uk/government/uploads/system/uploads/attachment_data/file/413234/No_place_for_bullying.pdf (accessed 12 January 2017).

Ofcom (2013) *Children and parents: Media use and attitudes report*. Available at: http://stakeholders.ofcom.org.uk/binaries/research/media-literacy/october-2013/research07Oct2013.pdf (accessed 7 January 2017).

Ofsted (2015a) *School inspection handbook*. Available at: www.gov.uk/government/publications/school-inspection-handbook-from-september-2015 (accessed 12 November 2016).

Ofsted (2015b) *Promoting positive body image within primary schools: Oak Cottage Primary School.* Available at: www.gov.uk/government/uploads/system/uploads/attachment_data/file/518021/Oak_Cottage_Primary_School_-_good_practice_example.pdf (accessed 3 February 2017).

Phippen, A. (2016) *360safe – The e-safety self review tool: UK schools online safety policy and practice assessment 2016.* Available at: www.swgfl.org.uk/360report2016.aspx (accessed 6 February 2017).

PSHE Association (2017) *Teacher guidance: Key standards in teaching about body image.* Available at: www.pshe-association.org.uk/curriculum-and-resources/resources/key-standards-teaching-about-body-image (accessed 6 February 2017).

PSHE Association Guidance (2015) Available at: www.pshe-association.org.uk/curriculum-and-resources/curriculum?CategoryID=1053 (accessed 6 February 2017).

The Royal College of Psychiatrists (2017) *The emotional cost of bullying: Information for parents, carers and anyone who works with young people.* Available at: www.rcpsych.ac.uk/healthadvice/parentsandyouthinfo/parentscarers/bullyingandemotion.aspx (accessed 27 January 2017).

Sharples, M., Graber, R., Harrison, C. and Logan, K. (2009) E-safety and Web 2.0 for children aged 11–16. *Journal of Computer Assisted Learning*, 25: 70–84.

Smith, P., Mahdavi, J., Carvalho, M. and Tippett, N. (2006) *An investigation into cyberbullying, its forms, awareness and impact, and the relationship between age and gender in cyberbullying.* Available at: http://webarchive.nationalarchives.gov.uk/20130401151715/http://www.education.gov.uk/publications/eOrderingDownload/RBX03-06.pdf (accessed 27 January 2017).

Stirling, S. and Emery, H. (2016) *A whole school framework for emotional well-being and mental health.* Available at: www.ncb.org.uk/sites/default/files/field/attachment/NCB%20School%20Well%20Being%20Framework%20Leaders%20Tool%20FINAL.pdf (accessed 9 August 2016).

Subrahmanyam, K. and Greenfield, P. (2008) Online communication and adolescent relationships. *The Future of Children,* 18: 119–146.

Tynes, B. (2007) Internet safety gone wild. *Journal of Adolescent Research,* 22: 575–584.

UNICEF (1992) *UN Convention on the Rights of the Child.* Available at: www.unicef.org/crc/files/Rights_overview.pdf (accessed 2 February 2017).

Valkenburg, P. and Peter, J. (2010) Online communication amongst adolescents: An integrated model of its attraction, opportunities and risks. *Journal of Adolescent Health,* 48: 121–127.

Yeager, D. and Dweck, C. (2012) Mindsets that promote resilience: When students believe that personal characteristics can be developed. *Educational Psychologist,* 47(4): 302–314.

6

THE INFLUENCE OF FAMILY MENTAL HEALTH

Chapter objectives

By the end of this chapter you should be aware of:

- the impact of maternal mental health in pregnancy and the early years and the potential impact on the developing child/young person and their emotional well-being;
- paternal mental health and the possible impact on the child/young person's mental health and emotional well-being;
- how family mental health difficulties can be translated into the classroom setting;
- how to develop an interagency approach to support families with mental health difficulties and the advantages of this approach to children and young people and the whole school;
- ways to engage with parents within a supportive framework.

Teachers' Standards

This chapter supports the development of the following Teachers' Standards:

TS8: Fulfil wider professional responsibilities

- Develop effective professional relationships with colleagues, knowing how and when to draw on advice and specialist support.
- Take responsibility for improving teaching through appropriate professional development, responding to advice and feedback from colleagues.
- Communicate effectively with parents with regard to pupils' achievements and well-being.

Introduction

This chapter will focus on the influence of family mental health in pregnancy, the early years and beyond in order to seek to understand the impact on the developing child/young person. How family mental health affects the child and then how this becomes translated into the classroom will also be explored. It will also consider the importance of engaging and working with parents who are affected by family mental health issues, demonstrating how an interagency approach could support family mental health. Further thought will be given to what an interagency approach could look like and the advantages to the family and the school of using such an approach in order to achieve high levels of engagment.

The prevalence and most common mental health difficulties within the family and the potential impact on the child

When considering the 'family' within this chapter, reference will be made, in the main, to parents. With one in four adults in the UK experiencing some form of mental illness in any given year (McManus et al., 2009) and many of these being parents, it is important that as professionals working with families we are aware of the most common types of mental illness in order to understand their impact on parents, children and young people. It is also important to consider that parental mental illness can vary in impact and the way that it presents itself and that the effect on the child is influenced by the type, severity and duration of the illness (Henry and Kumar, 1998, as cited by Aldridge and Becker, 2003). It can be evidenced that families from poorer and more disadvantaged backgrounds are more likely to be affected by common mental health difficulties (such as those listed below) and their adverse consequences (Campion et al., 2013). With approximately 17,000 children and young people in the UK living with parents with severe and enduring mental illness (Mental Health Foundation, 2016a), the need to support the family within an interagency approach has never been greater.

According to the National Institute for Health and Care Excellence (NICE, 2011) the most common adult mental health illnesses include depression and anxiety disorders (namely: generalised anxiety disorder, social anxiety disorder, panic disorder, obsessive-compulsive disorder (OCD) and post-traumatic stress disorder (PTSD)). In order to understand the impact on children and young people there is a need for an awareness of how mental health difficulties affect parents; you can find a brief synopsis and further information regarding specific common adult mental health difficulties at **www.time-to-change.org.uk/mental-health-and-stigma/types-mental-health-problems**.

Siblings of children/young people with a mental illness are individuals that have largely gone unrecognised and can remain invisible to statutory services. These children and young people will have unique experiences shaped by this relationship, and their mental health and well-being can be negatively affected by a number of factors (Greenberg et al., 1997). These negative factors include:

- increased responsibility within the family unit;

- possible loss of support from their sibling;

- changes in role (such as taking on new supportive roles);

- intense and conflicting emotions (for example confusion, despair, hopelessness, anger, and grief);

- interpersonal and intrapersonal difficulties;

- difficulties in trying to deal with the mental health system.

(Griffiths and Sin, 2016)

Stigma can also contribute negatively to siblings; if they tell others about their sibling's mental health they may receive support or they may be shunned, lose friends and experience discrimination – this makes for a difficult choice for those so young. Many siblings find that having a brother or sister with a mental illness is not always an exclusively negative experience. They can find great strength and compassion within their relationship that they can then apply to others; they also gain coping skills and knowledge that can benefit their own lives. These experiences can also lead to new opportunities and life directions (Jewell, 2000; Sin et al., 2008).

In terms of gender difference within parental mental health, women are more likely than men to have a common mental health difficulty (19.7 per cent as opposed to 12.5 per cent) (McManus et al., 2009). Women are also twice as likely as men to be diagnosed with anxiety disorders (Martin-Merino et al., 2009). However, men are over three times more likely to commit suicide than women (Oliffe et al., 2011) and men tend to exhibit mental health difficulties more indirectly, for example through alcohol and substance misuse, aggression towards themselves or others and risk-taking in general (DoH, 2012; Wilkins, 2010; Courtenay, 2000). Evidence suggests that larger numbers of men have undiagnosed mental health problems, this being due to stigma regarding mental health, societal constraints of masculinity, differences in presentations of mental illness and inappropriate services to support men (Devon, 2016). This is particularly the case when we consider the impact of mental health stigma towards black and minority ethnic communities, with 93 per cent of people surveyed indicating that they face discrimination because of their mental ill health (Owen, 2013). To further consider gender differences and the impact of family mental health difficulties on children and young people, the next few subsections will separate paternal and maternal mental health and highlight the impact on the family.

 KEY REFLECTIONS

- Why is it important that we have some awareness of the most common adult mental health difficulties?

- How can we ensure that the needs of siblings of children/young people with mental health difficulties are considered?

- How significant is the impact of mental health stigma on all family members, and in particular black and minority ethnic families?

Paternal mental health and the possible impact on the child/young person

To fully explore paternal mental health we initially need to think about what it is to be a father and how that role has changed dramatically over the past three decades from an all-powerful patriarch to a new nurturant father, who plays an active role in his children's lives (Lamb, 2004; O'Brien, 2005). Whereas previously, societal expectations would demand that the primary responsibility of child-care would fall to the mother, 69 per cent of parents now believe childcare is the responsibility of both parents (Ellison et al., 2009). Since 2003, unmarried fathers jointly registering their child's birth have the right to full parental responsibility; parental leave for fathers has also been extended (Gov. UK, 2014a, 2014b). This demonstrates society's current emphasis on preserving a child's relationship with their biological father. Government policy is being informed and underpinned by attachment theory and evidence regarding disadvantage facing children growing up in fatherless families, which in the main appears to be related to social and financial stresses (Trinder and Lamb, 2005). These changes are an indicator of a growing acknowledgment and recognition of the important role of a father in children's lives.

Research demonstrates that active and regular engagement of fathers in a child's life predicts a range of positive outcomes for children including reducing behavioural problems and psychosocial problems, enhancing cognitive development and decreasing the likelihood of involvement in crime (Sarkadi et al., 2007). There is a need, therefore, to support fathers in their role, to help them be prepared for changes to come and to support them in managing their own and their children's emotions and uncertainties, whether at home or in school.

Changes in the family structure and family functioning alongside increasing numbers of women in the workforce have raised questions about fathers' parenting-related stress and their mental health and how it may affect their children. There are numerous studies that suggest negative influences on parent–child interactions and children's development. It is important to note, however, that the majority of these studies focus on mothers. Harewood et al. (2016) indicate small to moderate effects of fathers' parenting-related stress on cognitive and language development in children aged 2–3 years with specific detrimental effects on boys' language development, even though the majority of fathers in the study were not primary carers. This study indicates that fathers have a direct effect on their children's development and suggests that interventions should address both mothers' and fathers' parenting-related stress and emotional health so they can better support their children's development (Harewood et al., 2016).

A recent campaign by Time to Change (2016) uncovered how teenage boys' own attitudes to mental health are influenced by their fathers' behaviour and their ability to talk about their feelings, with half of teenage boys feeling they cannot open up to their dads about their mental health. The emphasis of the campaign is to encourage fathers to talk more openly to their sons to empower them to successfully manage their own mental health (Censuswide, 2016). In relation to the early years there is a growing interest in understanding how a father's postnatal mental health influences outcomes for children in childhood. Ramchandani et al. (2005) associate fathers' postnatal depressive symptoms with emotional and behavioural difficulties for children aged 3–7 years and Fletcher et al. (2011) report that children whose fathers reported postnatal depressive symptoms were more likely to experience social, emotional and behavioural difficulties by age 5. These studies demonstrate the need for specific strategies and support for both parents in the postnatal and early years period for long-term investment in the well-being of their children throughout their lives and educational career.

Parental mental health is frequently cited as a feature in Serious Case Reviews, together with domestic abuse and substance misuse (frequently alcohol). This is often referred to as the 'toxic trio' and was evident in the Serious Case Review of Daniel Pelka. Daniel's mother had been diagnosed with clinical depression. She was also admitted to hospital and seen by mental health professionals following an overdose (Coventry Safeguarding Children Board, 2013). Serious Case Reviews like Daniel's indicate that professionals sometimes lack awareness of the extent that a mental health problem can impact on parenting capacity and how this can result in a failure to identify potential safeguarding issues. Therefore, learning from case reviews indicates that professionals, importantly those in education settings, must be able to recognise the relationship between adult mental health and child protection, maintaining focus on the child but also listening to parents, to be able to recognise risk. It is also important to recognise other issues such as drug or alcohol dependency, domestic violence and little or no family/community support in addition to mental health problems that can exacerbate the risk presented by mental health issues (Brandon et al., 2013). The majority of parents with mental health issues present no risk to their children but even in low-level concern cases the needs of the children must be paramount. The following case study can help you to think further about the impact of paternal mental health on children and supportive ways of working and services that may help.

CASE STUDY: JAMAL

Jamal is 9 years old and is currently in Year 4 at the local primary school. He lives with his dad, Tyrone, and his 5-year-old brother, Saul (in reception class). Tyrone struggles with depression, which can affect his parenting capacity and his ability to care for himself. The family are supported by Grandma Jean (Tyrone's mother) who lives nearby and visits daily to offer practical and emotional support to both boys and Tyrone. The family have a good relationship with the school and both boys' teachers, and Tyrone attends parents' evenings and assemblies when he and Grandma Jean are able to.

Teachers have noticed that over the past few weeks, both boys have been arriving to school late, appear hungry and are dishevelled, wearing unwashed/creased clothing. Jamal has said that dad is sleeping lots and Grandma Jean has been ill so not able to come as often to see them. During class the boys are tired and irritable which is very different to how they usually behave. When Tyrone collects the boys from school at the end of the day he swiftly takes them away and does not want to engage with anyone.

Case study reflections

- What are the major changes that have put the boys at risk?
- What should be the school's response to this situation?
- What can the school do to support the family at this time?

Jamal and Saul are vulnerable to their father's mental health and as such their recent behaviours and appearance are a significant concern and a sign that the family is not coping. Grandma Jean being ill and unable to help also means that the boys and Tyrone are subjected to further distress and uncertainty. The school has built up a good relationship with the family and should specifically try to engage Tyrone in a conversation urgently, either by phone or in person, to discuss their concerns regarding the children, the school's statutory role in supporting the children's health and well-being and the effects on the children's education. The children are at risk of neglect and there is an ongoing concern regarding their health and well-being whilst their father is ill and Grandma Jean is not well. Initially the school should try to meet with the family and engage them within a Common Assessment Framework (CAF)/Family Assessment Framework (FCAF)/Early Help to think further with them about interagency support that would help the situation. If this is not possible there needs to be a safeguarding referral made to children's social care services to undertake an assessment to think further about support for the family and specific help needed now and possibly in the future.

It would be good practice in this case to talk to Tyrone first to discuss the safeguarding referral, but if he refuses to engage or disagrees with the referral it should still go ahead as the children's safety and well-being must always come first, in accordance with safeguarding legislation and policy. Both Jamal and Saul need to be told that the teachers are worried about them and their dad, and are going to help and will be asking other professionals to help also. Jamal and Saul will need to be reassured that they have someone they can share their worries with, that they are being heard and things will get better, as they will be worried about their dad and missing their grandma and are doing the best they can in an uncertain environment. The school could invite the children to breakfast club and ensure their nutritional needs are met through the day. If this family is in receipt of pupil premium monies this could be used by the school to support the children's well-being as well as other aspects of their educational needs. Both Jamal and Saul should be given space and time to express their feelings and ask questions within a contained, supportive and safe environment.

Maternal mental health and the possible impact on the child/young person

Becoming a mother is a time of heightened emotions, and while most of these are positive, some women will experience temporary feelings of low mood, and there will be some women where these feelings may be severe and long-lasting. The mental health of women during pregnancy and within a year of giving birth (perinatal mental health) is a public health priority due to its impact on both the mother and the child's health. Statistics demonstrate around 50 per cent of perinatal mental health problems are untreated or undetected and this can have a devastating impact on women and their families (Mental Health Foundation, 2016b). There are several common mental health conditions during pregnancy, with depression being the most common. While most women experience 'baby blues' following delivery, postnatal psychological distress is highly prevalent across a variety of cultures (Satyanarayana et al., 2011). Research has also demonstrated a link between disadvantaged socioeconomic status and postnatal depression (Tannous et al., 2008).

The main impact of maternal mental health is on the attachment relationship between baby and mother and it is important to consider that bonding between a mother and her baby begins fairly early in pregnancy (Sedgmen et al., 2006). Maternal and paternal depression has been found to predict a difficult child temperament at 6–8 months and 21–24 months within a large cohort study (Avon Longitudinal Study of Parents and Children) and the effects were found to be more significant for boys than girls (Hanington et al., 2010). Murray et al. (2011) also reported an increased risk of depression in children and young people by age 16 whose mothers suffered from postnatal depression. Anxiety in mothers has also been found to predict a difficult infant temperament such as clinging behaviour, frequent crying and irritability (Austin et al., 2005).

Some studies have demonstrated a link between maternal depression and cognitive and language difficulties as the child gets older (Sohr-Preston and Scaramella, 2006); others, however, have found no evidence of such a relationship (Tse et al., 2010). Psychological distress and mental illness, including depression and anxiety, influence a child's emotional, cognitive and behaviour development (Hollins, 2007) with maternal depression that occurred when the child was 2–3 years old being a risk factor for anxiety in 10–11-year-olds (Letourneau, 2013). Studies have also demonstrated a link between maternal antenatal anxiety and attention deficit hyperactivity disorder (ADHD) in children, showing that if a mother is stressed whilst pregnant, her child is substantially more likely to have emotional or cognitive difficulties, including an increased risk of ADHD, anxiety and language delay (Van den Bergh et al., 2005).

There is also a well-established link between mental ill health and domestic violence and abuse, and both men and women, across all diagnoses, are more likely to have experienced domestic violence than the general population (Howard, 2012). The most prevalent cause of depression and other mental health difficulties in women is domestic violence and abuse, and it is estimated this is the case in 50–60 per cent of women mental health service users (Trevillion et al., 2012). Research such as this highlights the need for professionals to recognise the increased vulnerability of men and women with mental health difficulties to domestic violence and the implications of this for their children. Professionals require training and supervision to be able to identify and address these issues. Children and young people's needs remain paramount and it is important that

> *organisations must ensure that staff working with children always focus on the needs of the child, and never allow themselves to be distracted by the problems of the adults.*

> (Brandon et al., 2010)

Whilst reflecting on the possible effects of family mental health difficulties on a child/young person, as detailed above, it is also important to be aware of protective factors that can help to mediate some of these effects, such as:

- the mental ill health being mild or short-lived;

- there being another parent or family member who can help;

- there being no other family disharmony;

- the child/young person having wider support from extended family, friends, teachers or other adults;

- a secure base – the child/young person feeling a sense of belonging and security;

- the child/young person having good self-esteem – an internal sense of worth and competence;

- the child/young person having a sense of self-efficacy – a sense of mastery and control, along with an accurate understanding of personal strengths and limitations;

- there being at least one secure attachment relationship;

- there being access to wider supports such as extended family and friends;

- there are positive nursery, school and or community experiences.

(Greater Manchester Safeguarding Partnership, 2014)

The role of teachers, teaching staff and the school is evident within most of the above protective factors, offering a unique opportunity to support the child/young person and their family. Other chapters also examine how schools can support children and young people who have, or who may exhibit, issues around mental health and well-being. The following subsection will help you to think further as to how teaching staff in particular could engage the family and work together with other agencies to support the child/young person and their family.

Engaging families and encouraging a positive school climate

One protective factor to encourage good mental health in children and young people is the creation of a positive school environment that enhances a sense of belonging and connectedness (Public Health England, 2016). Weare (2015) promotes the importance of engaging the 'whole community' and building a supportive school with a sense of connectedness, focus and purpose, the acceptance of respect, warm relationships and positive communication and the celebration of difference. These concepts need to be applied to families, especially those with family mental health needs. Naomi (a parent of two, who struggles with anxiety) blogs about her experiences at her children's school:

School found out about my mental health difficulties when social services got involved. At the time I was humiliated and my mental health deteriorated but the school was amazing – without their gentle kindness and support my mental health would have remained unmanageable. They asked me how they could help and did all they could to reduce my anxiety and stress. They helped me meet with the local parenting programme where we sat with our knees against the tiny infant table. They agreed I could drop off and pick up ten minutes early. It made a huge difference to my anxiety and with that reduced I began thinking more clearly and began working on different ways to manage the playground situation and began making connections with other parents.

(Mind, 2015)

We can see from Naomi's blog post how valuable a positive and non-stigmatising approach can be in a school setting and how building a relationship with teaching staff based on kindness and support with small thoughtful changes and suggestions can make a big difference to families.

Working with families has been shown to have a significant impact on children and young people's mental health, both by helping family life reinforce the messages of the school and by helping parents to develop their own parenting skills and approaches (Weare, 2015). When working with families with mental health difficulties the 'whole school' should promote a non-stigmatising, non-judgemental approach so that parents do not feel blamed for their children's difficulties; schools must look for strengths in families and try to build on them. Some parents will have had a negative experience of school as children, so teachers will need an empathetic and thoughtful approach in order to encourage an accepting, trusting relationship to be established between the school and parents. It is vitally important that schools nurture a connectedness with parents or carers. This must be done very carefully, however, and sometimes very slowly. For example, this may start with schools or a class teacher encouraging parents to give up time to hear readers or help with cooking or craft sessions. This can be, for many, a non-threatening way to support building bridges between the work of the school and class and a parent. By getting parents involved in schools they can see all the good work that is done to support children and young people. They can start to build trusting relationships with professionals, which in the long term may prove invaluable in getting a family to accept and engage with support.

The importance of an interagency approach to support family mental health

Inter- or multi-agency approaches and ways of working have received much attention over the years, especially within the area of child protection. It has also been the focus of political agendas; Every Child Matters (HM Treasury, 2003), for example, set out a model of practice that involved a range of professionals working together in order to promote positive outcomes for children and young people. Even though this White Paper is no longer current governmental policy, the principles of using a multi-agency approach to encourage best practice and the best outcomes for the family still stand. In the context of education and family mental health in particular, an example of multi-agency working is the collaboration of services under a Common Assessment Framework (CAF) or Family Assessment Framework (FCAF) or Early Help. This framework encourages schools and all services to work together to meet the needs of a child/young person/family to ensure they have the opportunity to fulfil his/her/their potential. Effective multi-agency working can be a significant challenge; it is time-consuming and can lead to conflict. However, it significantly contributes to putting together different parts of the jigsaw and can lead to more effective services and joint problem-solving to the benefit of the child/young person and their family (Atkinson et al., 2007).

When working with families with multiple and complex problems and needs connected to parental mental health and safeguarding, the Think Family agenda (DCSF, 2009) is a useful framework to ensure a joined-up approach to these needs. This framework aims to give clarity to the roles and responsibilities of agencies to ensure co-operation and collaborative working. It works with family strengths, providing tailored support needs. Based on the Crossing Bridges Family Model (Falkov, 1998), the Think Family agenda helps professionals to consider the parent, the child and the family as a whole, and how the mental health and well-being of the family where a parent has a mental illness are linked in at least three ways:

1. Parental mental health problems can adversely affect the development, and in some cases, the safety, of children.

2. Growing up with a parent with a mental illness can have a negative impact on a person's adjustment in adulthood, including their transition to parenthood.

3. Children, particularly those with emotional, behavioural or chronic physical difficulties, can precipitate or exacerbate mental ill health in their parents/carers.

This framework is now considered ex-government policy but is still being used within many local authorities within England as a concept to recognise and promote the importance of a whole family approach, particularly within the agenda of parental mental health and child welfare.

 KEY REFLECTIONS

*   What could be the possible impacts on the child/young person when their parent has a mental illness and will all children/young people be affected and in the same way?
*   What protective factors mediate the effects of family mental illness and how could the school encourage these and what would that look like?

CHAPTER SUMMARY

*   A range of common mental health difficulties can exist within the family and these can have a significant impact on children and young people.
*   Adhering to statutory requirements with regard to safeguarding children and young people is important, and professionals need to be vigilant to the impact of changes within the family.
*   All teaching staff should be encouraging and supporting to parents within a 'positive community', encompassing a non-stigmatising and non-judgemental, strength-based approach.

FURTHER READING

Common Assessment Framework. Available at: www.education.gov.uk/consultations/downloadable Docs/ACFA006.pdf.

Family Action. Available at: www.family-action.org.uk/what-we-do/adult-mental-health-and-well being.

━━ REFERENCES ━━━━━━━━━━━━━━━━━━━━━━━━━━━

Aldridge, J. and Becker, S. (2003) *Children Caring for Parents with Mental Illness: Perspectives of Young Carers, Parents and Professionals.* Bristol: The Policy Press.

Atkinson, M., Jones, M. and Lamont, E. (2007) *Multi-agency working and its implications for practice: A review of the literature.* Available at: www.nfer.ac.uk/publications/MAD01/MAD01.pdf.

Austin, M.P., Hadzi-Pavlovic, D., Leader, L., Saint, K. and Parker, G. (2005) Maternal trait anxiety, depression and life event stress in pregnancy: Relationships with infant temperament. *Early Human Development*, 81: 183–190.

Brandon, M., Sidebotham, P., Bailey, S. and Belderson, P. (2010) *A study of recommendations arising from serious case reviews 2009–2010.* Available at: www.gov.uk/government/uploads/system/uploads/attach ment_data/file/182521/DFE-RR157.pdf.

Brandon, M., Bailey, S., Belderson, P. and Larsson, B. (2013) *Neglect and Serious Case Reviews: A report from the University of East Anglia,* commissioned by NSPCC. Available at: www.nspcc.org.uk/globalas sets/documents/research-reports/neglect-serious-case-reviews-report.pdf.

Campion, J., Bhugra, D., Bailey, S. and Marmot, M. (2013) Inequality and mental disorders: Opportunities for action. *The Lancet*, 382(9888): 183–184.

Censuswide (2016) *Time to change.* Available at: www.time-to-change.org.uk/news/half-teenage-boys-dont-feel-they-can-open-their-dads-about-mental-health.

Courtenay, W. (2000) Constructions of masculinity and their influence on men's well-being: A theory of gender and health. *Social Sciences and Medicine*, 50: 1385–1401.

Coventry Safeguarding Children Board (2013) *Daniel Pelka: Serious Case Review.* Available at: http://moderngov.coventry.gov.uk/documents/s13235/Daniel%20Pelka%20Serious%20Case%20 Review%20SCR.pdf.

Department of Health (DoH) (2012) *Statistics from the national drug treatment monitoring system: Vol 1, The numbers.* Available from: www.nta.nhs.uk/uploads/statisticsfromndtms201112vol1thenumbersfinal.pdf.

Devon, N. (2016) 'The male mental health crisis is real – so why is it still being ignored?' *The Telegraph* (4 February). Available at: www.telegraph.co.uk/men/thinking-man/the-male-mental-health-crisis-is-real–so-why-is-it-still-being/.

Ellison, G., Barker, A. and Kulasuriya, T. (2009) *Work and Care: A Study of Modern Parents.* Manchester: EHRC.

Falkov, A. (1998) *Crossing Bridges: Training Resources for Working with Mentally Ill Parents and their Children – Reader for Managers, Practitioners and Trainers.* Brighton: Pavilion Publishing.

Fletcher, R., Freeman, E., Garfield, C. and Vimpani, G. (2011) The effects of early paternal depression on children's development. *Medical Journal of Australia*, 195: 685–689.

Gov.UK (2014a) *Parental rights and responsibilities.* Available at: www.gov.uk/parental-rights-responsi bilities/who-has-parental-responsibility.

Gov.UK (2014b) *New shared parental leave regulations come into effect.* Available at: www.gov.uk/govern ment/news/new-shared-parental-leave-regulations-come-into-effect.

Greater Manchester Safeguarding Partnership (2014) *Children of parents with mental health difficulties.* Available at: http://greatermanchesterscb.proceduresonline.com/chapters/p_ch_par_mental_health_diff.html.

Greenberg, J.S., Kim, H.W. and Greenley, J.R. (1997). Factors associated with subjective burden in siblings of adults with severe mental illness. *American Journal of Orthopsychiatry*, 67: 231–241.

Griffiths, C. and Sin, J. (2016) Rethinking siblings and mental illness. *British Psychological Society*, 26: 808–811.

Hanington, L., Ramchandani, P. and Stein, A. (2010) Parental depression and child temperament: Assessing child to parent effects in a longitudinal population study. *Infant Behaviour & Development*, 33: 88–95.

Harewood, T., Vallotton, C. and Brophy-Herb, H. (2016) More than just the breadwinner: The effects of fathers' parenting stress on children's language and cognitive development. *Infant and Child Development*, 1–19. DOI: 10.1002/icd.1984.

HM Treasury (2003) *Every child matters* (Cm5860). Available at: www.gov.uk/government/publications/every-child-matters.

Hollins, K. (2007) Consequences of antenatal mental health problems for child health and development. *Current Opinions Obstetrics & Gynecology*, 1: 568–572.

Howard, L. (2012) *People with mental disorders more likely to have experienced domestic violence.* Available at: www.kcl.ac.uk/ioppn/news/records/2012/December/Domestic-violence.aspx.

Jewell, T.C. (2000) Impact of mental illness on well siblings: A sea of confusion. *Journal of the National Alliance on Mental Illness*, 11(2): 34–36.

Lamb, M. (2004) *The Role of the Father in Child Development.* Hoboken, NJ: John Wiley & Sons.

Letourneau, N. (2013) Maternal depression, family functioning and children's longitudinal development. *Journal of Pediatric Nursing*, 28(3): 223–234.

Martin-Merino, E., Ruigomez, A., Wallander, M., Johansson, S. and Garcia- Rodriguez, L. (2009) Prevalence, incidence, morbidity and treatment patterns in a cohort of patients diagnosed with anxiety in UK primary care. *Family Practice*, 27(1): 9–16.

McManus, S., Meltzer, H., Brugha, T., Bebbington, P. and Jenkins, R. (eds) (2009) *Adult psychiatric morbidity in England, 2007: Results of a household survey.* NHS Information Centre for Health and Social Care: 1–274. Available at: www.hscic.gov.uk/catalogue/PUB02931/adul-psyc-morb- res-hou-sur-eng-2007-rep.pdf.

Mental Health Foundation (2016a) *Parents.* Available at: www.mentalhealth.org.uk/a-to-z/p/parents.

Mental Health Foundation (2016b) *Mums and babies in mind.* Available at: www.mentalhealth.org.uk/projects/mums-and-babies-mind.

Mind (2015) Naomi (20 January): Mental health and the school playground. Available at: www.mind.org.uk/information-support/your-stories/mental-health-and-the-school-playground/#.WIEk7ztxvV4.

Murray, L., Arteche, A., Pasco Fearon, D., Halligan, S., Goodyer, I. and Cooper, P. (2011) Maternal postnatal depression and the development of depression in offspring up to 16 years of age. *Child & Adolescent Psychiatry*, 50(5): 460–470.

NICE (2011) *Common mental health disorders | Guidance and guidelines | NICE*. Available at: www.nice.org.uk/guidance/cg123.

O'Brien, M. (2005) *Shared Caring: Bringing Father into the Frame*. London: Equal Opportunities Commission.

Oliffe, J., Kelly, M. M., Bottorff, J. L., Johnson, J. L. and Wong, S. T. (2011) 'He's more typically female because he's not afraid to cry': Connecting heterosexual gender relations and men's depressions. *Social Science and Medicine*, 73(5): 775–782.

Owen, D. (2013) *Mental health survey of ethnic minorities*. Ethnos Research and Consultancy. Available at: www.time-to-change.org.uk/sites/default/files/TTC_Final%20Report_ETHNOS_summary_1.pdf.

Public Health England (2016) *The mental health of children and young people in England*. Available at: www.gov.uk/government/uploads/system/uploads/attachment_data/file/575632/Mental_health_of_children_in_England.pdf.

Ramchandani, P., Stein, A., Evans, J. and O'Connor, T. (2005) Paternal depression in the postnatal period and child development: A prospective population study. *The Lancet*, 365: 2201–2205.

Sarkadi, A., Kristinsson, R., Oberklaid, F. and Bremberg, S. (2007) Fathers' involvement and children's developmental outcomes: A systematic review of longitudinal studies. *Acta Paediatrica*, 97: 153–158.

Satyanarayana, V., Lukose, A. and Srinivasan, K. (2011) Maternal mental health in pregnancy and child behaviour. *Indian Journal of Psychiatry*, 53(4): 351–361.

Sedgmen, B., McMahon, C., Cairns, D., Benzie, R. and Woodfield, R. (2006) The impact of two-dimensional versus three-dimensional ultrasound exposure on maternal-fetal attachment and maternal health behavior in pregnancy. *Ultrasound in Obstetrics & Gynecology*, 27: 245–251.

Sin, J., Moone, N. and Harris, P. (2008). Siblings of individuals with first-episode psychosis: Understanding their experiences and needs. *Journal of Psychosocial Nursing*, 46(6): 34–38.

Sohr-Preston, S. and Scaramella, L. (2006) Implications of timing of maternal depressive symptoms for early cognitive and language development. *Clinical Child Family Psychology Review*, 9: 65–83.

Tannous, L., Gigante, L.P., Fuchs, S.C. and Busnello, E.D. (2008) Postnatal depression in Southern Brazil: Prevalence and its demographic and socioeconomic determinants. *BMC Psychiatry*, 8(1). DOI: 10.1186/1471-244X-8-1.

Trinder, L. and Lamb, M. (2005) Measuring up? The relationship between correlates of children's adjustment and both family law and policy in England. *Louisiana Law Review*, 56: 1509–1537.

Trevillion, K., Oram, S., Feder, G. and Howard, L. (2012) Experiences of domestic violence and mental disorders: A systematic review and meta-analysis. *Public Library of Science ONE*, 7(12). DOI: 10.1371/journal.pone.0051740.

Tse, A.C., Rich-Edwards, J.W., Rifas-Shiman, S.L., Gillman, M.W. and Oken, E. (2010) Association of maternal prenatal depressive symptoms with child cognition at age 3 years. *Paediatric Perinatal Epidemiology*, 24: 232–240.

Van den Bergh, B.R., Mennes, M., Oosterlaan, J., Stevens, V., Stiers, P. and Marcoen, A. (2005) High antenatal maternal anxiety is related to impulsivity during performance on cognitive tasks in 14- and 15-year-olds. *Neuroscience Bio behavioural Review*, 29: 259–269.

Weare, K. (2015) *What Works in Promoting Social and Emotional Well-being and Responding to Mental Health Problems in Schools?* London: National Children's Bureau.

Wilkins, D. (2010) *Untold Problems: A Review of the Essential Issues in the Mental Health of Men and Boys*. London: Men's Health Forum.

7
THE NEED FOR INCLUSION

Chapter objectives

By the end of this chapter you should be aware of:

- the concept of inclusivity in relation to children and young people's mental health and well-being in schools;
- the importance of applying inclusivity to a child or young person's mental health and well-being;
- the benefits of inclusivity to the child/young person, the school, staff and the wider community;
- the benefits of promoting an inclusive ethos towards children and young people's mental health and well-being in school;
- strategies that can support the promotion of an inclusive ethos within schools.

Teachers' Standards

This chapter supports the development of the following Teachers' Standards:

TS1: Set high expectations which inspire, motivate and challenge pupils

- Establish a safe and stimulating environment for pupils, rooted in mutual respect.
- Set goals that stretch and challenge pupils of all backgrounds, abilities and dispositions.

TS2: Promote good progress and outcomes by pupils

- Be aware of pupils' capabilities and their prior knowledge, and plan teaching to build on these.

TS5: Adapt teaching to respond to the strengths and needs of all pupils

- Know when and how to differentiate appropriately, using approaches which enable pupils to be taught effectively.
- Have a secure understanding of how a range of factors can inhibit pupils' ability to learn, and how best to overcome these.
- Demonstrate an awareness of the physical, social and intellectual development of children, and know how to adapt teaching to support pupils' education at different stages of development.
- Have a clear understanding of the needs of all pupils, including those with special educational needs; those of high ability; those with English as an additional language; those with disabilities; and be able to use and evaluate distinctive teaching approaches to engage and support them.

Introduction

This chapter will focus on the need to promote an inclusive ethos within schools when supporting children and young people's mental health and well-being. It will make links to the existing principle of inclusivity laid out within the Special Educational Needs and Disability (SEND) Code of Practice (Department for Education, 2015). It will examine the current concept of inclusivity within schools, both as an ethos in itself and in relation to legislation and guidance from both the Department for Education and Department of Health, and explore what this means for the promotion of children's mental health and well-being in schools. Consideration will be given to the benefits of inclusivity to the child or young person and the impact of this on the relationship with their school, staff and the wider community. Finally, the chapter will explore strategies that can support the promotion of an inclusive ethos for children and young people's mental health and well-being.

Defining inclusion and practice

The journey to define and understand the concept of inclusion has long been considered a lengthy and complex task. This has resulted in claims being made that inclusion forms a 'bewildering concept' which can allow for a range of applications and interpretation (Avramidis et al., 2002, p158). The task to define this notion has also been complicated by its inextricable link to our drive for understanding the concept of special educational needs and disabilities (SEND), especially given that such a concept has long been associated with that of a learning difficulty or a disability in line with the definition as set out by the Education Act 1996. This has meant that the mental health and well-being of children and young people has historically been somewhat marginalised when considering the notion of inclusion. This is surprising given that *The National Service Framework: Children, Young People and Maternity Services* (Department of Health, 2004) identified that 10 per cent of 5–15 year olds had a diagnosable mental health disorder. That is equivalent to three children in every classroom in every school in Britain. A further 15 per cent have less severe problems and remain at an increased risk of future mental health problems (Brown et al., 2012, cited in Department for Education, 2015, p34). *Future in Mind* (Department of Health, 2015) acknowledged 1 in 10 children needs support for mental health problems.

The notion that inclusive education has developed from what may be seen as a social model of disability, which recognises the difference in children, has led to this term's constant evolution in an attempt to reflect such differences (Save the Children, 2002). What seems important is not so much a definition of what is inclusion but the need to understand that inclusion is an ongoing process. This involves educators continually striving to meet such diverse needs through what may be seen as a constantly evolving and responsive set of pedagogies. Through our attempts to explore inclusive practice there has been more recently a greater impetus to explore the notion of inclusion in terms of what it means for the educational practice of children and young people. This has been driven by Acts of Parliament such as the Equality Act 2010, which made it unlawful for any education provider, including a private or independent provider, to discriminate between children and young people on the grounds of disability, race, sex, gender reassignment, pregnancy and maternity, religion or belief, or sex (known as 'protected characteristics'). Mental health difficulties are therefore now a protected characteristic under the 'disability' section of the Act, with its application being linked to whether the individuals have a physical or mental impairment that has a substantial, adverse and long term effect on your normal day-to-day activities. It is important to note that without a clinical diagnosis it may be unclear if a child falls under such a 'protected characteristic'. However, frequently nowadays children in schools are diagnosed with neurodevelopmental conditions such as attention deficit hyperactivity disorder (ADHD), autistic spectrum condition (ASC) or even perhaps a mental health condition such as depression or anxiety.

More recently with the Children and Families Act (2014) and the Special Educational Needs and Disability Code of Practice: 0 to 25 Years (Department for Education, 2015), inclusive policy and practice now truly acknowledges the importance of social, emotional and mental health difficulties within pupils in our schools. Whole school approaches aimed at promoting good mental health with all learners are now highlighted as best practice within government guidance, *Mental Health and Behaviour in Schools* (Department for Education, 2015). This guidance also contains useful examples of ways to achieve a whole school inclusive approach with regard to children and young people's mental health and well-being. This approach ensures an inclusive ethos to supporting mental health. It seeks to emphasise a preventative universal provision, rather than those which may been seen as reactive and targeted (Vostanis et al., 2012). It is worth noting, however, that there has been a historic profile of a separation between school and health and that child health has been a matter for local decision. In addition, there have been conflicts and challenges posed by those who are responsible for health on an individual level, for example *Choosing Health* (Department of Health, 2004), rather than that of the whole community. This includes families and schools, who have a responsibility as set out in the Extended Schools and Health Services programme (Department for Education and Skills/Department of Health, 2006; DeBelle et al., 2007).

Despite the journey we have been on to promote and establish inclusive practice, there will no doubt be future hurdles to overcome to establish best practice. However, as the United Nations Educational, Scientific and Cultural Organisation (UNESCO) notes, it is important that we are

> *proactive in identifying the barriers and obstacles learners encounter in attempting to access opportunities for quality education, as well as in removing those barriers and obstacles that lead to exclusion.*

(UNESCO, 2005, p13)

 KEY REFLECTIONS

- How has the notion of inclusion developed over time?
- How would you now define inclusion?
- Will the definition of inclusive practice continue to develop?

The importance of schools for the inclusion of children and young people's mental health and well-being

It is worth remembering that 'child and adolescent mental health' is a relatively new health care specialism following the *Together We Stand* document in 1995 (Health Advisory Service, 1995). Prior to that date, children in schools were often identified as problematic largely from a behaviour-based position, which still continues in part today. Teachers and support staff routinely study and take courses in behaviour management, yet children and young people's needs are very much more complex, especially those children with mental health problems. There is a need to redress the problem of specific training if children's mental health is to be placed on a similar footing as SEND. Schools traditionally have special educational needs co-ordinators (SENCo); in order to take a more inclusive approach to mental health in schools, however, there needs to be an extension of the SENCo role or an additional role created using staff who have a specialist interest in child and adolescent mental health. This would be in-keeping with recommendations set out in *Future in Mind* (Department of Health, 2015).

The most recent survey of children and young people's mental health in the UK was over a decade ago, meaning there is now a lack of reliable and up to date information (Health Select Committee, 2014) regarding statistical significance. Whilst recent research has indicated an increase in the number of children and young people with mental health difficulties, accurate research figures are important to ensure professionals are not working in a 'fog' and that provision both in schools and in the community is appropriate and timely. As stated by research, the current estimate is that 1 in 10 children and young people experience clinically significant mental health difficulties (Green et al., 2005; Maughan et al., 2005), with such figures being seen as being very similar to research in the USA (Waller et al., 2006). It is these children, young people and their families that will come into come into contact with schools, in the main, for support. Green et al. (2005) suggest that of the families that had sought help, nearly three quarters had first approached a teacher, in contrast with a quarter that had visited their family doctor. Greenberg (2010, p28) suggests:

> By virtue of their central role in lives of children and families and their broad reach, schools are the primary setting in which many initial concerns arise and can be effectively remediated.

Having access to supportive and understanding teachers can be very helpful for these children, young people and their parents given that the school setting will make up a significant proportion of the time in a child's life. It is very often at school where difficulties and problems are first noticed since teaching staff – the professionals who spend the longest contact time with children – are uniquely placed to inclusively foster mental health and well-being. Mental health and well-being also depends on teaching and support staff having a fundamental knowledge and understanding of infant and child development and the management of transitional stages. However, while expecting schools to focus on mental health, Weare (2000, p6) suggests:

it is not simply to add yet another demand to teacher's already impossible workload; effective social and affective education is directly beneficial to academic attainment and can therefore help teachers be more effective.

Previous government directives in England have increasingly emphasised the role of a public health approach, with schools being instrumental in the preventative work around mental health problems and promoting well-being – for example: *Every Child Matters* (Department for Education and Skills, 2003); *National Healthy Schools* (Department of Health/Department for Education and Employment, 1999) and *Social and Emotional Aspects of Learning* (Department for Education and Skills, 2005, 2006; Department for Children, Schools and Families, 2007). These policies and frameworks offered both universal and targeted mental health interventions and support. Targeting Mental Health in Schools (TaMHS) (Department for Children, Schools and Families, 2008) was rolled out from 2008 onwards and provided a much-needed framework through which local authorities could develop their own way of working, aiming to foster the role of schools in England in promoting children and young people's mental health. TaMHS was funded for three years between 2008–11 at some targeted schools and areas. It was well-received by school staff, including teachers, parents and pupils. Some schools have continued with and adopted aspects and principles of the project but there has been no consistent approach or monitoring since. Overall, successive governments have held differing priorities with a rather 'hotch potch' approach to projects instead of a longer term, universal and consistent approach. Despite the evidence to their effectiveness, there is no current appetite for the rolling out of universal implementation of projects such as TaMHS. Such a situation is even more worrying given the current government's proposal and direction for all schools in England to become academies where there will be individual interpretation of inclusivity regarding mental health and ways to support pupils.

As a result of research and government guidance, the theme of 'inclusion' and a move towards an emphasis on prevention of mental health difficulties rather than a reactive approach is now thought to be the way forward, as emphasised within *Mental Health and Behaviour in Schools, Departmental Advice for School Staff* (Department for Education, 2015). For children and young people there is a strong correlation between mental health issues in childhood and those within adulthood. Research suggests that figures equate to 50 per cent of young adults with mental health difficulties having been diagnosed between the ages of 11 and 15 (Kim-Cohen et al., 2003). Over half of lifetime mental health problems (excluding dementia) begin to emerge by age 14 and three-quarters by the mid-20s. Up to 80 per cent of adults with depression and anxiety disorders first experience them before the age of 18 (Department of Health, 2011, 2015). Therefore, early identification and support for mental health and well-being within primary schools for all children and young people is of particular importance. It could be suggested that universal mental health provision within schools offers the ability to 'immunise' children and young people from later difficulties (Merrell and Gueldner, 2010). This 'immunisation' potential is closely linked to the potential protective factors from improving resilience as discussed in Chapter 4. Rutter (1991), in addition to his work on resilience, showed that school experiences are not just important for educational attainment, but also for psychological development. Greenberg (2010) suggests that a universal 'inclusion-based' approach also reduces the potential for stigmatising participants. With these thoughts in mind, a review of 599 primary schools and 137 secondary schools and their emotional health promotion strategies cited that although two thirds of schools' approaches focused on all pupils, these were still largely reactive rather than preventative interventions (Vostanis et al., 2012). This study suggests that we have some way to go before a totally inclusive approach to promoting mental health and well-being for children and young people in schools is realised.

The benefits of inclusivity to the child/young person, the school, staff and the wider community

The following case study aims to provide an insight into the benefits of inclusivity to the child/young person, the school and the wider community. Consider ideas for practice around inclusion and mental health with this example in mind.

 CASE STUDY: JENNY

Jenny is 11 and has moved into a new county to join a Year 6 class in an urban primary school. Her attendance has been sporadic. Jenny has previously been presented to child and adolescent mental health services following an act of self-harm. Jenny's education experience has included several exclusions following events of unacceptable behaviour in class. She has been subject to numerous school moves including three primary schools. Jenny is not able to tell the time on the clock and says she cannot read beyond a very basic level. She is unhappy about this and wishes things were different. Jenny's ethnic and cultural background is Gypsy/Traveller. Jenny and her family are settled Travellers and though they have moved to a new house they are again on the point of eviction. Jenny's sister, who is 17, has just had a baby and has returned to live in the family home. Her younger brother has a diagnosis of ADHD and is also violent at times. Jenny's older brother is away at college. Her parents are together; Mum has recently had a health scare but has just had the all clear.

Case study reflections

- What were the major factors that put Jenny at risk?
- What can the school do to support this situation?

Jenny is an example of a young person trying to deal with multiple layers of problems and has been left with an overwhelming sense of hopelessness. One way she has managed her incapacity to read is through behaving badly as that worked in a way to remove her from what was, for Jenny, an intolerable situation, especially as she grew older and it became clearer she was behind her peers. She is now even more isolated from any peers that she was friendly with. Unless Jenny's parents disclose their Traveller status on admission to their new school it may be some time before the school can access advisory support services which seek to improve the outcomes for Gypsy, Roma and Traveller (GRT) children and families.

The school may wish to seek an urgent referral to their integrated behaviour outreach team or social inclusion officer in order to seek the best outcomes for Jenny. This may alert the school to the previous child and adolescent mental health services (CAMHS) referral. Given her low levels of academic achievement, the school will need to do all it can, in consultation with their SENCo, to liaise with her prior settings as to what strategies may best support her needs. Jenny will need a lot of support given her complex needs and will require assigned and targeted support to help her cope in class. They will need to quickly understand what is driving her previous levels of poor behaviour so that the most appropriate interventions can be put in place.

Inclusive practice in schools

Having a positive inclusive school climate will in part be mainly dependent on the individual leadership from both the head teachers and governors. However, having said this, schools have a statutory responsibility for creating a teaching and learning environment which is inclusive no matter what the child's needs may be, whether they are defined by physical, ethnic, gender or with regard to social, emotional and mental health needs. Every school should make clear reference in their school policy how they intend to admit and support the equality, diversity and inclusion of those children with such needs in their school. This is in order to create a supportive, appropriate and purposeful teaching and learning environment. Such policies will have been informed by two key pieces of legislation. The Equality Act 2010 clearly sets out the legal obligations that schools have towards their children and young people. This includes not discriminating, harassing or victimising such groups as well as making reasonable adjustments to ensure that such individuals are not disadvantaged. The Special Educational Needs and Disability Code of Practice: 0 to 25 Years (Department for Education, 2015) highlights how a range of needs can be assessed and supported. It helps schools to acknowledge in their inclusive policy and practice the importance of social, emotional and mental health difficulties within pupils. It allows schools to consider a whole school approach to supporting such needs by identifying the issues schools face when supporting such vulnerable individuals. These include

> *becoming withdrawn or isolated, as well as displaying challenging, disruptive or disturbing behaviour ... anxiety or depression, self-harming, substance misuse, eating disorders or physical symptoms that are medically unexplained. Other children and young people may have disorders such as attention deficit disorder, attention deficit hyperactive disorder or attachment disorder.*

> (Department for Education, 2015, p98)

Strategies for inclusive practice in schools

For any inclusive school-based strategy to be successful it is important for educational professionals to understand the relationship between the child, their family, school and the wider community. The 'Extended Schools' initiative, which commenced in 2001, was very much about embedding schools as part of their wider community and using them as a resource for their communities as a longer term agenda. Principal messages were about making parents and families welcome, engaging health and social care professionals in the school setting, including child and adolescent mental health professionals, and participation in community activities (DeBelle et al., 2007).

Children often receive a home visit from the class teacher prior to starting primary school. This is a really helpful way of making home and family links and for school staff to see their pupils within a context. It also eases the transition for starting school for both family and child and helps to build a firm foundation for future relationship-building. It is now common practice to have breakfast clubs in schools as well as after school clubs. These are a good example of promoting inclusivity as they are open to all children. After school clubs provide opportunities for children to engage in extra-curricular activities often of a non-academic nature such as sports, music and cookery. They provide further opportunities for children who may not find the classroom an easy place to excel in, to do so in another area. Positive family and friendship relationships scaffold a child's experience of life; this can also be said of positive relationships in the school setting with peers and school staff. Before and after school clubs often expose children to additional staff outside their classrooms with opportunities for further positive relationships to develop. Other supportive strategies include developing friendships and social networks through having similar characteristics and shared common interests.

CASE STUDY: AMID

Amid is 7 and he has just joined Year 3. He has struggled somewhat with his academic work in Key Stage 1 but the school has not in the past been overly concerned about Amid. However, with his move to Key Stage 2 he is becoming more aware of how he is not like his peers academically. This has meant he is now reluctant to work and has a sense that he is no good at anything. To avoid work and to garner popularity with his class friends he is starting to disrupt the lessons by calling out and disturbing others on the carpet. The school are becoming more and concerned that he is falling behind his classmates and allied with his disruptive nature the staff are concerned for his future.

Case study reflections

- What factors are influencing Amid's behaviour?
- Do you think his behaviour will continue to deteriorate?
- What can the school do to support Amid?

Usually, before a range of interventions and support are put in place for children like Amid, the school must assess his level of SEND and linked to this his emotional and mental health needs. In order to achieve this, an initial assessment will take place to ascertain how Amid's needs may be best supported given his move to Key Stage 2. This assessment has originated from concerns from his new teacher who has started to share her concerns regarding his progress, actions and behaviours with the SENCo and Amid's parents. This assessment will now take a more formal route which will include a full analysis of Amid's needs, the views of his parents being sought and teacher assessments and observations being made. Parents must be informed before any SEND intervention can be implemented for Amid. Early interventions can often prevent any emotional issues from escalating so it is important that swift action is taken. It is also important that whatever the school does, it forms part of what may be seen as a graduated approach to support inclusion.

A graduated response

Initially interventions may take the form of strategies linked to what is known as 'quality first teaching'. Such strategies provide a safe, happy and welcoming school environment so that all children can flourish. For any aspects of inclusive practice to be effective all practitioners need to buy into the belief that all children are important and that they deserve the best educational opportunities and care. They must model inclusive values by being accepting and open to the range of needs given the many stresses that may be brought to the situation.

Strategies to support aspects of inclusion can include developing the culture of the classroom, adapting teaching styles and methods, adopting a range of access strategies, and supplying additional class-based support or making referrals.

Developing the culture of the classroom

- Put in place agreed, acceptable and negotiated ground rules for any undesirable behaviour. Often it will be necessary for a consistency of approach to be maintained to promote progress with children with social, emotional and mental health difficulties. Despite the needs, everyone should be clear about the non-negotiables for unacceptable behaviour such as harming others.

- Making children feel valued and raising their self-esteem through giving them class-based responsibilities, promoting success in the curriculum and through the use of SEAL scheme circle time activities.

- The promotion of a 'can do' culture within the classroom and school, where all children's work is displayed and all forms of achievement are acknowledged. For children who have behavioural needs as a result of any of their issues that social success is valued just as highly as academic prowess.

- Giving the child a 'voice' where children are listened to and no concerns will be dismissed.

- A culture of accepting difference. Children with particular needs may not wish to work as a group and may prefer to work individually. They may have short attention spans or they may become angry and disruptive. Children may need to be given the space and time to calm down or a safe place to go to until they are ready to be reintegrated into activities. The systems in the classroom and school need to be flexible enough to support such needs whilst minimising the disruption to all other pupils.

Adapting teaching styles and methods

As part of a school's drive to include pupils whatever their need, it is important that the child's work is structured to support them and to move them from the known to unknown items that are achievable. Sometimes learning objectives may have to be changed to take into account the need so that a child is able to succeed in order to build self-esteem as well as improve levels of motivation to continue with any work. Some work will need to be modified in light of potential triggers that can take a child into less desirable moods or emotions, for example asking a child to write about a birthday party or best friend when a child has experienced isolation from friends and family. For some children, strategies such as pre-teaching words or concepts prior to a lesson beginning may lead to a greater involvement of children in the lessons, facilitating success as well as reducing aspects of negative self-esteem regarding a child's academic prowess as well as providing reassurance that they can engage in the lesson. Teachers may also wish to find alternative ways to support children to record their ideas, such as taking photographs or use of a teaching assistant (TA) as a scribe.

Adopting a range of access strategies

Many schools now adopt a range of inclusive access strategies in relation to children and young people's mental health and well-being in schools. These include:

- Visual timetables to reassure pupils who are anxious or have short term memory issues. Visual timetables can be used so that children are provided with the security of knowing what each day or lesson may hold for them.

- Simple auditory meter displays, which a child can access to show when the noise in class may be too high, and can support pupils with limited social skills or children on the autism spectrum.

- The use of stress balls and fidgets to help pupils with autism or ADHD focus and seek a means to manage the stress during their school day. These simple and effective toys allow pupils to engage their hands and fingers in movement rather than them distracting others in the class or when on the carpet.

- Access to supportive resources such as number lines, word mats and working walls.

- Emotion cards so that children who may find difficulty in verbalising their emotions can inform adults of their needs to be left alone since they may be angry or sad.

Additional school-based support or referrals

Under the new SEND code of practice, schools are required to hold a record of the level of need/register, indicating the level of need a child may face with regard to their SEND. If a child is failing to make progress and there is a marked deterioration in any of their needs after using class-based support strategies, a more graduated, focused approach may be taken by the school. This will mean the children may be placed on the register needing 'SEN support' which will involve taking actions to remove any further barriers to learning and to put relevant special educational provision in place.

Working together, the teacher, SENCo and parents may create a 'provision map' for the child to map out the interventions that may be used over a particular timeframe. As part of developing this, a school may seek input from a specialist agency such as an educational psychologist. They will further assess a child's needs and suggest other agencies or a support package that may be carried out by a trained TA linked to the provision map. For example this may lead to work being deemed necessary on developing a child's social and emotional skills. Targeted interventions such as 'socially speaking', involving the children in a board game which helps them focus on listening skills, social interactions and the pupils' ability to develop and use receptive and expressive language. By interacting with a range of social scenarios – such as, if a child keeps interrupting when another child wishes to speak – children are given the opportunity to practise skills such as taking turns and how best to go about achieving the best outcomes.

Such activities can help children negotiate more challenging situations whilst also diminishing the chance of riskier behaviours escalating from situations. Carrying out group social skills interventions in school can also mean that schools can address concerns relative to the school setting (Kasari et al., 2016). Other agencies such as the CAMHS or a child's general practitioner (GP) might also be accessed to help support a child's needs in school. Some schools may make use of a 'nurture group' as a means of providing a short term, focused intervention which seeks to remove barriers to learning as a result of social, emotional or behavioural difficulties (SEBD). Though the child or young person continues to remain a part of their own class, opportunities to join this group in school provide a safe, nurturing environment which seeks to foster positive relationships with both teachers and the child's peers. Finally, if parents are in agreement, a Common Assessment Framework (CAF) may also be initiated to support a co-ordinated effort to support a child's inclusion in school and possibly reduce the likelihood of an exclusion from school.

If after all other avenues of support within school are exhausted and the child still exhibits severe causes of concern for the school and/or parents, they may need to seek through the local authority a needs assessment to review the education and health care of the child. If successful, this review may lead to securing statutory funding for the child's educational future through an Education, Health and Care (EHC) Plan.

KEY REFLECTIONS

- What strategies can a class teacher employ to support the range of a pupil's needs?
- How might parents support the school to help their child?
- What can a school do to promote the inclusion of pupils with concerns?

CHAPTER SUMMARY

- Inclusion is an evolving concept linked to the concept of special educational needs.
- Inclusive practice supports pupils with mental health and well-being needs alongside a range of physical and learning needs.
- Schools have statutory duties to secure the inclusion of pupils with mental health and well-being needs.
- Successful inclusion involves working with parents.
- The school should respond to supporting pupils using graduated means.
- 'Quality first teaching' can form the basis for class-based inclusion.
- Schools may need to seek the help of outside agencies to promote inclusion.
- Funding can be sought to support a child's mental health and well-being needs if the school cannot support them using their own school budget.

FURTHER READING

Atkinson, M. and Hornby, G. (2002) *Mental Health Handbook for Schools.* London: Routledge.

Goepel, J., Childerhouse, H. and Sharpe, S. (2015) *Inclusive Primary Teaching.* 2nd edition. Northwich: Critical Publishing.

Glazzard, J., Stokoe, J., Hughes, A., Netherwood, A. and Neve, L. (2015) *Teaching and Supporting Children with Special Educational Needs and Disabilities in Primary Schools.* 2nd edition. London: SAGE/ Learning Matters.

REFERENCES

Avramidis, E., Bayliss, P. and Burden, R. (2002) Inclusion in action: An in-depth case study of an inclusive secondary school in the south-west of England. *International Journal of Inclusive Education,* 6(2): 143–163.

DeBelle, D., Buttigieg, M., Sherwin, S. and Lowe, K. (2007) The school as location for health promotion, in DeBelle, D. (ed.) *Public Health Practice & The School Age Population.* London: Edward Arnold.

Department for Children, Schools and Families (2007) *Social and Emotional Aspects of Learning (SEAL) programme: Guidance for secondary schools.* Nottingham: DCSF.

Department for Children, Schools and Families (2008) *Targeted Mental Health in Schools Project.* Nottingham: DCSF.

Department for Education (2015) *Mental health and behaviour in schools.* Available at: www.gov. uk/government/uploads/system/uploads/attachment_data/file/416786/Mental_Health_and_ Behaviour_-_Information_and_Tools_for_Schools_240515.pdf (accessed 15 February 2016).

Department for Education (2015) *Special educational needs and disability code of practice: 0 to 25 years.* Available at: www.gov.uk/government/uploads/system/uploads/attachment_data/file/398815/SEND_ Code_of_Practice_January_2015.pdf (accessed 15 February 2016).

Department for Education and Skills (2003) *Every child matters.* Nottingham: DfES.

Department for Education and Skills (2005) *Primary Social and Emotional Aspects of Learning (SEAL): Guidance for schools.* Nottingham: DfES.

Department for Education and Skills (2006) *Excellence and enjoyment: Social and Emotional Aspects of Learning (Key Stage 2 small group activities).* Nottingham: DfES.

Department for Education and Skills/Department of Health (2006) *Extended schools and health services: Working together for better outcomes for children and families.* London: CSIP.

Department of Health/Department for Education and Employment (1999) *National healthy schools programme.* Nottingham: DfEE.

Department of Health (2004) *National service framework: Children, young people and maternity services: The mental health and psychological wellbeing of children and young people,* Standard 9. Available at:

www.gov.uk/government/uploads/system/uploads/attachment_data/file/199959/National_Service_Framework_for_Children_Young_People_and_Maternity_Services_-_The_Mental_Health__and_Psychological_Well-being_of_Children_and_Young_People.pdf (accessed 1 April 2016).

Department of Health (2011) *No health without mental health: A cross government mental health outcomes strategy for people of all ages*. Available at: www.dh.gov.uk/en/Publicationsandstatistics/Publications/PublicationsPolicyAndGuidance/DH_123766 (accessed 1 April 2016)

Department of Health (2015) *Future in mind: Promoting and improving our children and young people's mental health and wellbeing*. Available at: www.gov.uk/government/uploads/system/uploads/attach ment_data/file/414024/Childrens_Mental_Health.pdf (accessed 15 February 2016).

Green, H., McGinnity, A., Meltzer, H., Ford, T. and Goodman, R. (2005) *Mental health of children and young people in Great Britain, 2004. A survey carried out by the Office for National Statistics on behalf of the Department of Health and the Scottish Executive*. Basingstoke: Palgrave Macmillan. Available at: www.hscic.gov.uk/catalogue/PUB06116/ment-heal-chil-youn-peop-gb-2004-rep2.pdf (accessed 15 February 2016).

Greenberg, M. (2010) School-based prevention: Current status and future challenges. *Effective Education*, 2: 27–52.

Health Advisory Service (1995) *'Together We Stand': The commissioning, role and management of child and adolescent mental health services*. London: HMSO.

Health Select Committee (2014) *Children's and adolescent's mental health services and CAMHS*. Available at: www.publications.parliament.uk/pa/cm201415/cmselect/cmhealth/342/34202.htm (accessed 15 February 2016).

Kasari, C., Dean, M., Kretzmann, M., Shih, W., Orlich, F., Whitney, R., Landa, R., Lord, C. and King, B. (2016) Children with autism spectrum disorder and social skills groups at school: A random-ized trial and comparing approach and peer composition. *Journal of Child Psychology and Psychiatry*, 57(2): 171–179.

Kim-Cohen, J., Caspi, A., Mot, T.E., Harrington, H., Milne, B.J. and Poulton, R. (2003) Prior juvenile diagnoses in adults with mental disorder: Developmental follow-back of a prospective longitudinal cohort. *Archives of General Psychiatry*, 60: 709–771.

Maughan, B., Iervolino, A. and Collishaw, S. (2005) Time trends in child and adolescent mental disorders. *Current Opinion in Psychiatry*, 18: 381–385.

Merrell, K. and Gueldner, B. (2010) *Social and Emotional Learning in the Classroom: Promoting Mental Health and Academic Success*. London: Guildford.

Rutter, M. (1991) Pathways from childhood to adult life: The role of schooling. *Pastoral Care in Education*, 9(3): 3–10.

Save the Children (2002) *Schools for all*. Available at: www.eenet.org.uk/resources/docs/schools_for_all.pdf (accessed 15 February 2016).

UNESCO (2005) *Ensuring access to education for all*. Available at: http://unesdoc.unesco.org/images/0014/001402/140224e.pdf (accessed 24 February 2016).

Vostanis, P., Humphrey, N., Fitzgerald, N., Deighton, J. and Wolpert, M. (2012) How do schools promote emotional well-being among their pupils? Findings from a national scoping survey of mental health provision in English schools. *Child and Adolescent Mental Health,* 18(3): 151–157.

Waller, R.J., Bresson, D.J. and Waller, K.S. (2006) The educator's role in child and adolescent mental health, in Waller, R.J. (ed.) *Fostering Child and Adolescent Mental Health in the Classroom.* Thousand Oaks, CA: SAGE.

Weare, K. (2000) *Promoting Mental, Emotional and Social Health.* London: Routledge.

8

WHO'S LOOKING
AFTER WHOM?

Chapter objectives

By the end of this chapter you should be aware of:

- the current issues relating to the mental health and well-being of educational professionals;
- how leaders can seek to understand and support professionals within their setting with regard to their own mental health and well-being;
- how schools can support resilience amongst professional staff;
- what outside agencies are available to support schools;
- how leaders can help and support a return to work for their staff given a period of prolonged illness.

Teachers' Standards

This chapter supports the development of the following Teachers' Standards:

TS8: Fulfil wider professional responsibilities

- Make a positive contribution to the wider life and ethos of the school.
- Develop effective professional relationships with colleagues, knowing how and when to draw on advice and specialist support.

Introduction

This chapter will focus on the current levels of mental health and well-being issues linked to the educational workforce and to those new to the profession. It will examine the risk factors associated with generating such health conditions as well as considering the impact it has on individuals' educational settings

The current situation

The mental health and well-being of children and young people has more recently become a major topic of concern in UK primary schools. This has resulted in a raft of advice and guidance coming from many agencies within education and health, with publications including the Department of Health (2015) *Future in Mind: Promoting, protecting and improving our children and young people's mental health and wellbeing.*

Alongside the concern that has been raised for children's long term well-being, there has been an emerging realisation of the influence that this has on the lives of the professionals working with them. Such influences can extend to all professionals whether new, or those longer established members of staff. Ongoing mental health and well-being concerns may present in a school's staff in the form of low-level anxiety, seasonal affective disorder and phobias. Many issues may have developed as a direct result of the impact of work-related pressures, including factors such as pupil behaviour, the pressures and demands being currently placed on educational professionals and the lack of funding to support them when dealing with the large range of needs of pupils presenting in schools currently. The research of Tyers et al. (2009) sought to identify six major components of stress in the workplace. These include workload demands, the level of an individual's ability to influence their working conditions, how change is managed, levels of support provided, relationships and an ability to understand their role.

The impact of these issues may not only be felt in terms of an individual's own personal health and staff absence but also in relation to their ongoing effectiveness and commitment as educational practitioners. Work by Day et al. (2006) has clearly shown the influence that interactions around a teacher's sense of well-being and work/life balance can have on their effectiveness, their sense of a teacher's commitment and the impact this can have on pupil progress. Furthermore, statistics from the Chartered Institute of Personnel and Development (CIPD, 2015) provide evidence of the clear link between professional absence and health-related illness. CIPD (2015) indicates that out of the five most common causes of long term absence for non-manual workers, stress-related absence was the highest of all factors with public sector workers. In this case, 79 per cent of absences reported were due to stress, compared to 58 per cent as a sector average. Recent statistics reported by Bloom (2016) indicate that 84 per cent of the 2,000 teachers sampled in a study by the Education Support Partnership (ESP) had suffered from mental health problems over a period of the last two years. This report also suggested that the numbers of teachers who have had mental health problems has risen over the last five years. As concerning was the suggestion that such impact upon professionals' health was leading high levels of teachers considering leaving the profession.

These rising figures are not surprising given that 1 in 4 adults will experience a mental health problem during their lifetime, to varying degrees. Mental health disorders are one of the leading causes of ill health and disability worldwide, with two-thirds of people never seeking help due to stigma and potential discrimination (World Health Organisation, 2001; MIND, 2013). Looking after those who look after and educate our children and young people has to be a priority.

Demands of workload

A range of workplace factors, such as the setting's health and safety practices, can obviously impact upon an individual's health and well-being (Patterson, 1997). Undoubtedly, as Garner (2016) indicates through the work of the ESP, teacher workload is a major factor of teaching professionals' mental health issues. For some of those new to the profession, such high levels of workload may come as an unwelcome surprise compared to those who have been in the profession for a longer period and who have had time to adapt and change to cope with such demands. These high levels of workload have led to many teachers feeling stressed, which has ultimately resulted in their feeling anxious and depressed. Given the constant level of public scrutiny through items such as the current inspection regime, it is not unexpected that surveys such as that conducted by the Association of Teachers and Lecturers in 2014 should draw links to damaged mental health and well-being resulting from the now constant inspections of schools and a culture of target-setting (Ratcliffe, 2014). However, such claims are not without their critics, who suggest that the attribution of blaming others should be avoided by school leaders (Richardson, 2012). Most worrying, however, is the revelation that 68 per cent of teachers who stated that they had experienced mental health issues had not informed employers of their conditions (Ratcliffe, 2014), which tends to be in line with above World Health Organisation commentary around stigma.

Levels of support

Another major factor that has been attributed to a diminished level of professional mental health and well-being is the level of access to support and training available to support pupils in any teacher's care. Well-being and mental health issues have been linked to coping with parental separation, substance abuse and domestic violence. Work undertaken by the National Foundation for Educational Research (NFER) for the Department for Education (DfE, 2014) studied schools' abilities to respond to issues relating to mental health in children and young people. They concluded that primary schools were less able to supply the provision needed to support pupils' mental health compared to that of secondary schools. Though teachers felt well-equipped to identify pupil behaviour linked to an issue around pupils' mental health, most concerning was that 32 per cent of respondents felt they had not been appropriately trained to identify mental health problems among pupils. Furthermore, class teachers felt that compared to senior leaders they were less likely to know how to help such individuals.

The National Association of Head Teachers (NAHT) published a survey in 2016 outlining the concerns of teachers, which suggests that over 10 per cent of pupils have a mental health problem before they are aged 11 (Richardson, 2016; NAHT/Place2Be, 2016). This is further evidenced in the British Child and Adolescent Mental Health Survey in 1999 and 2004 where it was identified that amongst 5–10-year-olds, 10 per cent of boys and 5 per cent of girls had mental health problems. For 11–16-year-olds the prevalence was 13 per cent for boys and 10 per cent for girls. The most common problems for this age group are attention deficit hyperactivity disorder (ADHD), anxiety and depression and autistic spectrum conditions (Murphy and Fonagy, 2012). All of these will manifest with potential problems in classrooms impacting on concentration and learning potential, together with the quality of the overall school day. Of the 1,455 English head teachers in the NAHT/Place2Be (2016) report sample, two-thirds of those in primary schools felt they were unable to deal with such issues. This was attributed to lack of resources despite the government claims of £1.4 billion funding being available for children's mental health.

For any teacher new to the profession, such reports will no doubt form the basis of professional concerns and anxiety. Such concerns will no doubt be exacerbated by the level of training that their course may have provided them with in how to deal with issues around mental health and well-being, coupled with their having just left university and the demands placed on them in terms of their new professional roles and responsibilities.

Given all of these contributing factors that link to the state of health and well-being of educational professionals in schools, it is important that this issue is addressed to support the many workers new to the profession or those who are more experienced who may find themselves potentially at risk as a result of the work they do in schools. This duty of care is more than that of a moral imperative as it forms part of the statutory duty of care placed upon employers regarding their employees under the Equality Act 2010 (UK.Gov, 2013). This Act clearly states that individuals may be deemed to have a disability if they have a physical or mental impairment that can have a substantial, adverse, long term effect clearly on their normal daily working lives. It is also the duty of the employer to make 'reasonable adjustments' so that the individual can do, and progress in, their job. Therefore, feel reassured that as a teacher you will not be alone should you be faced with any issues around dealing with your own mental health and well-being. Not only are there statutory duties placed on employers to support you, but given the caring nature of the profession no doubt if you have any concerns your colleagues will do their best to support your future needs.

KEY REFLECTIONS

- What influences can mental health and well-being have on educational professionals?
- What are the main contributing factors to teachers' mental health issues?

The role of leaders

As any educational professional should realise, the mental health and well-being of any employee must start from the very top of any school organisation. This will involve the head teachers, senior leaders and governors creating a culture in your school where the duty of care for safeguarding individuals is seen as of paramount importance. It is their responsibility that staff are deployed effectively and in the best interest of the setting, giving due regard to individuals having a reasonable work/life balance. The leadership team should make certain that you and all employees should feel that you should not suffer in silence, that there is someone that can be approached given any concerns no matter how small, and that there will be no stigma attached to any individuals admitting to work-related symptoms linked to mental health and well-being. As Weare (2016, p7) suggests:

It is helpful if the school climate and ethos routinely acknowledges the reality of staff stress and finds ways to make it safe for staff and leaders (as well as pupils) to acknowledge their human distress, weakness and difficulty and seek support and help for their mental health needs in non-stigmatising ways.

If you do not seek help this will inevitably lead to deterioration in your health so obtaining help and advice at the earliest of times is vital. Though there are many factors that can lead to teachers suffering mental health issues, many of these being associated with stress in the workplace, it is important to realise that all individuals deal with stress differently. It is also important for an individual to remember that 'stress' is 'normal' according to one's own acceptable levels of stress – without it we would not get up in the morning. However, some people are able to continue to work without realising the signs that they are becoming too stressed. It can be reassuring to you to note that your senior staff who lead you in your settings are not themselves exempt from stress. However, what is important is that a school should have some mechanism in place to help and support any individual if they have any concerns and worries.

It is therefore important for you to realise that the common signs of stress can make people act in a particular way, as shown below.

Signs of stress	Behaviours	Physical symptoms
Feeling anxious	Picking at the body, avoidance behaviours, becoming overly attached to a safety object/person	Panic attacks, chest pains, shortness of breath, sweaty palms, racing heart, sleep disturbance/fatigue, diarrhoea
Feeling depressed	Tearful, crying, not wanting to get up or go to work, lack of concentration at and during work	Physically feeling tired, waking early, headaches, loss or change of appetite
Feeling isolated/lonely	Feelings that no one likes you or that they do not wish to talk to you. Feelings that everyone is against you. Not wanting to talk to others, finding somewhere out of others' way	Feeling depressed, sad, lethargic
Feeling a sense of dread/unhappy	Feeling down about things, not seeing the positives in life and not happy to laugh or make light of things	Morbid feelings, tearful or crying
Feeling overloaded with work	Confusion, poor memory	Unable to sleep, waking early, mood swings, withdrawn, increased smoking or drinking 'to cope'
Feeling disinterested	Loss of drive for life and the job	Lethargy, lack of willingness to engage with the world and work
Feeling irritable	Not willing to listen to others, or restless	Snappy, being short tempered with people, impatient

To help leaders in schools identify the levels of stress that their staff are suffering, stress audits could be carried out. This may go some way to address the school's legal obligation to individuals, as with other employers, to make an appropriate and suitable assessment of the risks to the health and safety of their employees. This type of audit may help leaders understand the types and levels of stress that exist in their particular workplace and may help them see where individuals' issues are coming from. To take an audit you may be required to fill in a questionnaire and the results are then used to seek improvements in the areas of concern identified. In addition to this the school leaders may monitor staff sickness/absence through a monitoring policy so as to start to positively identify if there are any staff absences that may need a supporting investigation.

 KEY REFLECTIONS

- How are you currently feeling about work?
- What signs might you need to look for to gauge your mental health and well-being?
- Who in school might you feel comfortable talking to regarding any issues you may have?

Managing work-related stress

The following case study aims to provide an insight into the sort of pressures a teacher can face and how it can impact upon their mental health and well-being. Read the case study and consider ideas for practice strategies to support this person.

 CASE STUDY: SUNIL

Being responsible for the SATs, I feel personally responsible for each of the children and their results. I have started to feel sick and anxious when I think about it, and I am now shouting at my close friends and they are getting worried about me. They worry about the way I will react and this is also making me feel anxious. Given the parents I have it has all got very competitive. Also, with the result trends from last year, I know that we need some good results to show an upward progress with regard to children in writing. I am trying not to put pressure on the children but I find that I spend my evenings marking practice papers and analysing them to see how I can target work for each child to improve. I am finding I am waking up in the night thinking about things and when I think about it I am getting anxious. I am trying not to let it all get me down.

Case study reflections

- What are the triggers for Sunil's feelings towards his work?
- Who should he be sharing his feelings with?

Sunil is clearly being affected by the pressures placed on him at work. It is starting to affect his own health and the health of others around him. If he does not seek help this feeling will only grow and so will his isolation and levels of discontentment with his lot in life. The first step he must take is to realise he needs help before things get even worse for him. He must start by realising he is not alone and must talk to someone. This realisation is not a judgement on Sunil as a professional, or a sign of weakness, but a much-needed heightened awareness that, due to the pressure of work, he is struggling to cope. It may be worth considering that there are probably other staff in a similar position. He might not feel that he can talk to the staff or his head teacher at school since he may not wish to signal his own fallibility; if this is the case he should see his doctor. Hopefully the head teacher may have become aware of Sunil's fragile nature and if this is the case he might try and speak to him to signpost him to places for help.

Supporting well-being and fostering resilience

It is important that any school setting provide an environment that nurtures and promotes a sense of control over professional work and workload as well as providing means by which resilience can be nurtured amongst colleagues and groups of employees. As Weare (2016, p7) suggests:

> Schools need to ensure staff experience connection, through celebrating and sharing everyday successes and achievements, and are encouraged to know when to let go, to make more realistic demands on themselves, and have the kind of work/life balance that can help them recover and recuperate from the full-on nature of everyday school life.

Weare's (2016) suggestions around celebrating skills and achievements work for adults and professionals in relation to the work setting, in the same way as they do for children and young people, are discussed in Chapter 4. By improving resilience factors, risk factors have the potential to be minimised. You will find each school setting will have its own particular strategies to support their staff in their particular context. Some strategies that schools and leaders might consider suggesting include:

- Encouraging a climate where staff are encouraged to be able to share worries and concerns. This could be done at an individual level through an individual's own self-identified network within schools or meetings where concerns about the impact of new initiatives are shared.

- Allowing staff to attend training outside of their schools so they can meet with other colleagues to share experiences and to build up a different support network who they can also turn to when things get tough. This continuing professional development (CPD) could be related to a curriculum responsibility or interest or an academic qualification such as a Master's degree. Some courses could also be identified to support issues around workload or classroom management. Further support can be found in courses run by relevant unions, and again such attendance can be a means to build up a support network for individuals.

- Encouraging staff to do what can be done now and not later. Try and avoid 'busy work' which has no real purpose beyond making you feel better because you are doing things.

- Trying to organise times when staff are clearly valued and can be together. Perhaps on a Friday, organise cake or sandwiches to be made available in the staff room and make certain you say to all the staff this is a time for them and you want them to come no matter what. Show them it is important by giving clear signals that they are more important than that last task.

- Trying to dedicate a space in the school for a quiet area where staff can just go and not hear about work. Perhaps it can be a place where, if the school is committed to staff's well-being, an activity such as meditation could take place.

- Consider supporting opportunities for 'supervision' for all staff. 'Clinical' supervision is a mandatory, not a 'luxury', feature and an aspect of work for clinicians in practice, but is less practised in education settings. It can, however, provide a supportive, reflective and restorative framework (Andrews, 2016). Teaching staff similarly deal with difficult situations with pupils which are stressful and impact on the self and person; it can be helpful to create a thinking space with a respected colleague.

- Formalised peer mentoring or 'buddy' systems. Teaching staff are very good at formalising these supporting strategies for their pupils with good evidence to their effectiveness. Why not consider implementing similar systems across staff teams? This fits with the Teachers' Standards (2011, p13) 'develop effective professional relationships with colleagues'.

As Gardner (1993) suggests in his theory around multiple intelligences, there are many facets found within individuals that will impact upon a person's professional and personal life. Goleman (1996) also suggests that emotional intelligence can influence a person's ability to be self-aware with regard to knowing how they are feeling, whether they can handle such feelings and also control their level of motivation. Given this, it is important that you take notice of how you are feeling in your daily life, since such positive or negative feelings will have a profound influence on your ability to do the job and your mental health and well-being. Such scrutiny of one's feelings may also, in turn, provide a cue to signify that something must be done to mediate against any reductions in positive emotions towards the job and an individual's life in general.

For any staff maintaining a work/life balance will often provide the key to greater resilience against stress. It is important that you find times when you are free from thinking about the job in hand in order to spend time with family and friends or to take up a sport or hobby. No doubt some of the greatest barriers to all of this are excuses such as 'being tired' or it being 'too expensive', but remember there is always a way around this. If you feel tired, build up your commitment or find a time when you feel that doing this activity is most likely to happen. If things are too expensive try and find something for free such as a walk in the countryside.

Though everybody's work patterns will be different, try and set yourself a clear timetable of slots of time when you will not be on task or tempted to dip into work. This may be, for example, that you work up till 6 p.m. on a Friday and then start looking at work again at an agreed time on Sunday – though this is easier said than done given that sometimes things will get in the way, and sometimes you will be your own worst enemy. Nobody is indispensable and surely it is better you do your job well rather than on half a tank of energy or mental ability.

The practice of mindfulness offers the opportunity to foster inner resilience. It is being aware of and focused on what we are doing in the here and now, monitoring experiences in a non-judgemental way

(Kabat-Zin, 1994 as cited in Jennings, 2015). Mindfulness has been proven to enhance emotional self-regulation, increasing a sense of well-being and self-efficacy. Early research demonstrates that when used by teachers, it can also increase their ability to manage classroom behaviour and improve relationships with others (Meiklejohn et al., 2012). Nurturing a teacher's resilience using mindfulness-based training can also create a relational foundation in the classroom, in so much as it offers pupils, by default, mindful skills that nurture their own inner resilience. It is important to be aware that mindfulness is a skill that has to be practised regularly and over a period of time to fully realise its benefit. Mindfulness activities and training courses are widely available through a variety of means, such as self-help books, online training courses and those requiring attendance. Mindfulness practice is recommended by the National Institute for Health and Care Excellence (NICE) for reoccurring symptoms of depression (National Institute for Health and Care Excellence, 2016). It is also used in a variety of ways within the NHS to relieve symptoms of sleep problems, headaches, depression and for stress reduction (King's College Hospital NHS Foundation Trust & Guys and St Thomas' NHS Foundation Trust, 2013). More information regarding mindfulness practice and its benefits can be found at **https://mindfulnessinschools.org**.

Outside agency support for schools

Despite some leaders' and schools' best efforts in supporting you and their staff with issues around mental health and well-being, these concerns may not always be resolved at school level. In this case or with an extended period of absence due to illness, the school may need to access specialist agency support to support you, such as occupational health, to help with an individual's issues.

Normally most schools will have paid into a school level agreement (SLA) to buy in such an agency if required. Such services, as a matter of course, should be clearly signposted in schools to any individuals, alongside any other organisations such as unions who can help and advise you given any such issues. This specialist support could come through an approved medical practitioner or even a member of staff's own doctor. The benefits of such support may be centred on the objective, specialist overview that such practitioners can provide to best meet the needs of each individual.

If the employer should start to be concerned about your mental health and well-being, they should seek your agreement, so that they can make a referral to such agencies as soon as possible. They will need an individual's written consent before any other medical practitioner is allowed to access confidential medical records when being involved in such a case. You should be given a chance to understand the process that they are embarking on as well as why you think this is important for you. Often, given such conditions, any suggestions to access support may cause an individual to feel irritated, agitated or even victimised. However, if this is case and you have any concerns, you should remind yourself that they are suggesting this for your well-being; such a referral should be encouraged and seen as a positive move to support you. It should be seen as a means of offering specialist support by a professional who understands the cause and impact of such issues upon both your personal and professional life. It will provide a specialist who can understand your condition as well as suggesting or signposting treatments that may support your recovery. If you are off on sick-leave, then such agencies can also suggest some ways of offering you a phased return to work. It is important to note, however, that the work of these services is advisory. Normally a report will be sent to the human resources department linked to the local authority. The report will include a return to work date, advice for the employer to support your recovery/return to work and any reasonable adjustments that could be made to support your condition when at work. Since the report does not produce statutory guidance it is the decision of the employer whether to act on or take up this advice.

Other agencies that can provide you with support could include the person's union and those shown below.

Organisational overview	Website link
The Health and Safety Executive provides a range of useful links and guidance linked to matters surrounding health and safety.	**www.hse.gov.uk/stress/ mymental.htm**
The FitforWork website provides access to a range of occupational health professionals who can offer advice and support around work-based issues.	**http://fitforwork.org/ employee**
Anxiety UK provides information and support for those with anxiety disorders.	**www.anxietyuk.org.uk/**
The Samaritans provides free confidential advice and support.	**www.samaritans.org/**
Mind is a mental health charity.	**www.mind.org.uk/**
The Mental Health Foundation provides guidance and research around issues relating to mental health.	**www.mentalhealth. org.uk/**
Time to Change challenges mental health stigma and discrimination.	**www.time-to-change. org.uk/about-us**

Reasonable adjustments

Your setting should realise and comply with the Equality Act 2010 with regard to making reasonable adjustments to help those individuals who have developed a long term mental health issue which has been longer than 12 months, or who have an existing mental health issue. It is also important that your setting publishes information to demonstrate how they are complying with the Public Sector Equality Duty.

Reasonable adjustments will mean that your setting will have to make certain that any disabled workers are not disadvantaged compared to non-disabled workers as a result of the setting's policy, procedures or practice.

Such adjustments can involve:

- adjustments to the physical working environment;

- a reallocation of some duties to other individuals;

- changes to the individual's working practices or hours;

- support from trained individuals, mentor support or counselling.

It is important that you, as the employee, are consulted with regard to how you feel you can be best supported upon your return to work. Such measures must be seen by the employee as being supportive rather than punitive.

It is important, however, that when assessing if reasonable adjustments can be made that you realise that the employer will need to bear in mind the extent to which such adjustments are practical. This may include the financial costs or the extent to which such adjustments may cause internal disruption.

Following some conditions, a phased return to work may be considered as an option to support your return to work. This could include you taking part in a job-share arrangement with an internal colleague or having someone who has been employed to help support you in your daily duties. This option may include making adjustments in the form of flexible working hours, such as mornings only to start with. Extra class-based support may be introduced or a suggestion made that additional duties can be avoided, such as clubs or supervision at break times.

Given the ongoing stresses related to your mental health condition in such situations, it might be appropriate that the school suggests that you also find some form of advocacy to support or help you during this difficult time. This could be someone you get on with at work, a friend or family member. If this is not an option, information can be sought regarding the help and support you may get from organisations such as Mind or Mind Infoline. Given what may be for you a time of ongoing fragile mental health, an advocate may help you by being there to listen, in confidence. This may help you to perhaps see things more objectively and therefore you may feel in a better position to explore options with the person, or they may signpost you to legal support. Such support may help you to make the right informed decision, and, if needed, the advocate may accompany you to meetings as a means of additional support.

CASE STUDY: TARA

Tara has been struggling with her work, which has manifested itself with weeklong bouts of sickness absence. She has opened up to her manager, who has now persuaded Tara to go and see her doctor to discuss her worries around her work-related depression and feelings of anxiety with regard to her ability to cope with her job on a day to day basis. She has now been issued with a fit note by her doctor and she has handed this in to her setting. Tara has been signed off sick for a month.

Case study reflections

- What can the setting do to support her?
- What can be done to help her return to work?

Given Tara's ongoing ill health, the likelihood is that some adjustments will need to be made to support her return to work. It is important that an agreed line of communication between the setting and Tara is set up so that she is not left feeling isolated. The school could seek her agreement to attend a referral to occupational health to better understand and assess the barriers that are now stopping Tara from working. As soon as Tara is considered fit for some form of return to work, she will need to arrange a return to work meeting so that an agreed strategy can be put in place to support her return. Tara may feel that she needs the support of an advocate to help her through this process. The result of the return to work meeting may be a phased return or some support plan being put in place. It is important that this is mutually agreeable given the setting's limitations.

Ill health retirement

Unfortunately, even following the best efforts of everyone involved, sometimes a solution cannot be found to make a return to work possible. If this is the case, for you or any individual, it may be that ill health retirement is the only option now available. This will signal that you are now permanently incapable of carrying out your normal duties due to ill health. This should not be seen as defeat but a means by which you can still have a good quality of life freed from the burdens that may have led to your health issues. Sometimes the occupational health service can suggest that individuals might consider ill health retirement. Remember that you or any individual can decide to apply for such an option as long as you have got your doctor's or even a consultant's support. In such situations, it is anticipated that the setting manager will support the application so that they comply with the relevant statutory duties. An application will need to be made to either the Teachers' Pension Scheme or Local Government Pension Scheme in order to set this process in motion by the employer or individual as required by the relevant scheme.

KEY REFLECTIONS

- What are some of the key risk factors that can trigger issues around mental health and well-being?
- What strategies can schools and leaders put in place to support their staff?
- What outside agency support is available to a school and its staff with regard to issues around mental health and well-being?
- How can a school and leaders support a return to work for those individuals who may have suffered longer term illness?

CHAPTER SUMMARY

- Mental health and well-being issues can be triggered by a range of factors found in a professional's working life.
- Mental health and well-being issues can influence individuals' physical well-being.
- Schools have statutory duties to secure and include their staff with mental health and well-being needs.
- Providing clear strategies to support individuals and a climate of openness and no stigma is vital to reducing the isolation felt by staff with mental health and well-being issues.
- Provision of strategies should come from a 'top-down' approach that becomes embedded in the school system.
- Outside agencies can support schools and leaders who have issues around staff's mental health and well-being.
- Schools should find ways to support a return to work if there is long term illness.

—— FURTHER READING ——————————

A Guide to Mental Health. Available at: www.publichealth.hscni.net/sites/default/files/Mind_Your_Head_Booklet_LR_08_15_0.pdf (accessed 16 August 2016).

Healthy Schools. Guidance for Schools on Developing Emotional Health and Wellbeing. Available at: www.healthyschools.london.gov.uk/sites/default/files/EHWB.pdf (accessed 24 August 2016).

Workplace. Available at http://mind.org.uk/workplace (accessed 25 August 2016).

—— REFERENCES ——————————

Andrews, L. (2016) 'Family nurse partnership: why supervision matters'. *Nursing Times* (25 January). Available from: www.nursingtimes.net/roles/nurse-educators/family-nurse-partnership-why-supervision-matters/7001826.article (accessed 9 June 2016).

Bloom, A. (2016) *8 in 10 teachers have had mental-health problems and workload to blame*. Available at: www.tes.com/news/school-news/breaking-news/eight-10-teachers-have-had-mental-health-problems-and-workload-blame (accessed 7 April 2016).

Chartered Institute of Personnel and Development (2015) Absence Management Annual Survey Report 2015. Available at: www.cipd.co.uk/binaries/absence-management_2015.pdf (accessed 23 April 2016).

Day, C., Stobart, G., Sammons, P., Kington, A., Gu, Q., Smees, R. and Mujtaba, T. (2006) *Variations in Teachers' Work, Lives and Effectiveness*. London: Department for Education and Skills.

DfE (2014) *NFER teacher voice omnibus: Questions for the Department for Education – March to May 2014 and May to June 2014*. www.gov.uk/government/uploads/system/uploads/attachment_data/file/363735/RB391_-_NFER_Teacher_Voice_Omnibus.pdf (accessed 29 April 2016).

Department of Health (2015) *Future in mind: Promoting and improving our children and young people's mental health and wellbeing*. Available at: www.gov.uk/government/uploads/system/uploads/attachment_data/file/414024/Childrens_Mental_Health.pdf (accessed 15 February 2016).

Equality Act 2010. Available at: www.legislation.gov.uk/ukpga/2010/15/contents (accessed 23 July 2016).

Garner, R. (2016) 'Inside the "Samaritans for teachers" hotline that shows just how stressful the classroom can be'. *The Independent*. Available at: www.independent.co.uk/news/education/education-news/education-support-partnership-samaritans-for-teachers-hotline-that-shows-just-how-stressful-the-a6798136.html (accessed 8 April 2016).

Goleman, D. (1996) *Emotional Intelligence: Why It Can Matter More Than IQ*. London: Bloomsbury.

Jennings, P. (2015) *Mindfulness for Teachers*. W. W. Norton & Company: New York.

King's College Hospital NHS Foundation Trust & Guys and St Thomas' NHS Foundation Trust (2013) *Mindfulness-based stress reduction (MBSR)*. Available at: www.guysandstthomas.nhs.uk/resources/patient-information/elderly-care/mindfulness-based-stress-reduction.pdf (accessed 28 July 2016).

Meiklejohn, J., Philips, C., Freedman, M., Griffin, M., Biegel, G., Roach, A., Frank, J., Burke, C., Pinger, L., Soloway, G., Isberg, R., Sibinga, E., Grossman, L. and Saltzman, A. (2012) Integrating mindfulness training into K–12 education: Fostering the resilience of teachers and students. *Mindfulness*. DOI: 10.1007/s12671-012-0094-5.

MIND (2013) *Mental health facts and statistics*. Available at: www.mind.org.uk/information-support/types-of-mental-health-problems/statistics-and-facts-about-mental-health/how-common-are-mental-health-problems (accessed 29 July 2016).

Murphy, M. and Fonagy, P. (2012) Mental health problems in children and young people, in Annual Report of the Chief Medical Officer (2012) *Our children deserve better: Prevention pays*. Available at: www.gov.uk/government/uploads/system/uploads/attachment_data/file/252660/33571_2901304_CMO_Chapter_10.pdf (accessed 29 July 2016).

NAHT/Place2Be (2016) *Children's mental health matters: Provision of primary school counselling*. Available at: http://website.place2be.org.uk/media/10046/Childrens_Mental_Health_Week_2016_report.pdf (accessed 9 February 2017)

National Institute for Health and Care Excellence (2016) *Depression in adults: Recognition and management*. Available at: www.nice.org.uk/guidance/cg90?unlid=4306996020163922547 (accessed 28 July 2016).

Patterson, J.M. (1997). Vpp companies' best practices. *Occupational Health & Safety*, 66: 60–61.

Ratcliffe, R. (2014) 'Ofsted inspections and targets harming teachers' mental health, finds survey'. *The Guardian* (14 April). Available at: www.theguardian.com/education/2014/apr/14/ofsted-inspections-targets-harming-teachers-mental-health (accessed 15 April 2016).

Richardson, H. (2012) 'Ofsted chief Sir Michael Wilshaw: Teachers not stressed'. *BBC News*. Available at: www.bbc.co.uk/news/education-18025202 (accessed 11 April 2016).

Richardson, H. (2016) 'Heads warn over pupils' untreated mental health issues'. *BBC News*. Available at: www.bbc.co.uk/news/education-35502394 (accessed 24 April 2016).

Tyers, C., Broughton, A., Denvir, A., Wilson, S. and O'Ragan, S. (2009) *Organisational Responses to the HSE Management Standards for Work-related Stress: Progress of the Sector Implementation Plan Phase 1, Research Report RR693*. London: Health and Safety Executive.

UK.Gov (2013) Equality Act 2010: Guidance. Available at: www.gov.uk/guidance/equality-act-2010-guidance (accessed 12 February 2016).

Weare, K. (2015) *What Works in Promoting Social and Emotional Well-being and Responding to Mental Health Problems in School?* London: National Children's Bureau.

World Health Organisation (2001) *Mental disorders affect one in four people*. Available at: www.who.int/whr/2001/media_centre/press_release/en (accessed 29 July 2016).

INDEX

acceptance 32
access strategies 127
'acting out' 4, 45–6
ADHD (attention deficit hyperactivity disorder) 8–9
   access strategies 127
   case studies 14–15, 68, 69–70
   characteristics 8, 9, 46
   classroom strategies 46
   and conduct disorder 7
   environmental factors 9, 68, 109
   genetic influences 9, 68
   lifetime impairments 8
   positive aspects 10
   prevalence 6, 8, 135
   treatment 13
adolescent behaviour 5, 7, 11
after school clubs 74, 125
alcohol issues 35
anorexia nervosa 10
anti-social behaviour 8
anxiety 6–7, 135
   in adults 104, 109
   behaviour 47
   case study 16–17
   reasons for 5, 45, 46
Anxiety UK 142
ASC see autistic spectrum conditions
Asperger's Syndrome 9
assessment for learning 36
Association of Teachers and Lecturers (ATL) 47, 135
attachment 46, 106
   difficulties/disorder 5, 6, 46
   and maternal mental health 109
   and separation anxiety 7
attendance 30, 77
attention deficit hyperactivity disorder see ADHD
attention problems 45
autistic spectrum conditions (ASC) 9–10
   access strategies 127
   characteristics 10
   positive aspects 10
   prevalence 6, 8, 135
   SEND Code of Practice 56
autonomy 7
Avon Longitudinal Study of Parents and Children 109
Avramidis, E. et al. 119

Bandura, A. 64, 97
Banerjee, R. et al. 27
behaviour 43–4
   'acting out' 4, 45–6
   adolescent behaviour 5, 7, 11
   case studies 49, 52–3, 58–9

cause for concern 45–7
changes of behaviour 5, 6
context 5
disruptive behaviour 17–18
punishment for poor behaviour 4–5, 46
as reaction to adversity 5
risk factors 45
risk-taking behaviours 5
triggers 11, 51
behaviour policy 47–59
   barriers to relationships 50–3
   bullying 28, 30, 34, 87, 91
   levels of support 59
   nurture groups 53–5
   SEND code of practice 56–9
   strategies 48, 57
behavioural techniques 13
Bell, D. 11
Bennathan, M. 53
BEREAL 92, 95
bereavement 11, 65, 72
   counselling 39, 59
BESD see social, emotional and behavioural
   difficulties (SEBD)
Bloom, A. 134
Bloom's Taxonomy 96
BLP (Building Learning Power) 95
body image
   case study 94
   impact of social media 91–3
   and PSHE curriculum 93–5
Boxall Profile 53–4
Brain Gym 34
Brandon, M. et al. 109
breakfast clubs 54, 108, 125
British Child and Adolescent Mental Health Survey 135
Brooks, F. 26, 27
buddy systems 13–14
Building Learning Power (BLP) 95
bullying 83–4, 85–90
   cyberbullying 26–7, 37, 88–90
   defined 85
   feedback boxes 75
   impact of 11, 86
   prevalence 65, 85
   record-keeping 86–7
   and resilience 87–8
   whole school policy 28, 30, 34, 87, 91
   zero tolerance approach 87

CAF see Common Assessment Framework
CAMHS (child and adolescent mental health
   services) 3, 12, 13, 14, 15, 37, 75

care, duty of 47, 51, 136
carers *see* looked after children; parents,
    carers and families
case studies
    ADHD 14–15, 68, 69–70
    anxiety 16–17
    behaviour 49, 52–3, 58–9
    body image 94
    building resilience 95–6
    disruptive behaviour 17–18
    inclusivity 123–4, 125
    nurture groups 55
    paternal mental health 107–8
    self-efficacy 70–2
    self-esteem 49
    work-related stress 138–9, 143
CentreForum Commission 3
Chartered Institute of Personnel and
    Development (CIPD) 134
Child Exploitation and Online Protection
    Command (CEOP) 37
child health 120
child sexual exploitation (CSE) 37
ChildLine 64
Childnet International 89–90
Children and Families Act (2014) 120
Children and Young People's Mental Health and
    Wellbeing Taskforce 3
Children's Commissioner 85, 89
circle of friends 36–7
circle time 13, 32, 33–4, 54, 75, 76–7, 126
citizenship curriculum 34
classroom ethos, culture and environment 32, 48, 126
Claxton, G. 95
Clickers 95
'Closing the Gap' 95
cognitive behavioural therapy (CBT) 12, 13
Cole, T. 36, 37, 45, 47, 51
Common Assessment Framework (CAF) 108, 111, 128
communication difficulties 8
Communications Act (2003) 89
community involvement 30
comorbidity 5, 7
concentration, poor 8, 9, 13
conduct disorders 7–8
    characteristics 7
    comorbidity 7
    parenting practices 8
    prevalence 6, 7, 45
    risk factors 7–8
    treatment 13
congruence 13
context 5–6, 13, 15–16
continuing professional development (CPD)
    37–8, 51, 139
counselling 15–16
Cowie, H. *et al.* 27
critical incidents 59
Crossing Bridges Family Model 112

CSE (child sexual exploitation) 37
curriculum planning and practice 33–5
cyberbullying 26–7, 88–90
    CEOP training 37
    illegality of 89
    prevalence of 26, 88
    proactive measures 89–90

Day, C. *et al.* 134
Department for Education (DfE) 73, 75, 86, 88
    Mental health and behaviour in schools 26, 36, 39,
        47, 50, 91, 120, 122
Department of Health 27, 120
    see also 'Future in Mind'
depression 6, 47, 68, 135
    in adults 104, 109
    postnatal depression 106, 108, 109
DfES 76
Diagnostic Statistical Manual (DSM-5) 6, 7, 9
difference 73, 126
digital literacy 90
discrimination 86, 91, 105, 119–20, 124
disruptive behaviour 17–18
diversity 32
    see also inclusion; inclusive practice in schools
domestic violence and abuse 11, 107, 109
dramatherapy 97
drug education 30, 34, 35
duty of care 47, 51, 136
Dweck, C. 87–8

Early Help 111
eating
    change in pattern 6
    disorders 10
    mealtimes 54
Education Act (1996) 119
Education Act (2011) 89
Education, Health and Care (EHC) Plans 56,
        57–8, 128
Education Policy Institute 38
Education Support Partnership (ESP) 134, 135
Emery, H. 27, 30–1
emotional disorders 6–7
emotional intelligence 33, 76, 140
emotional literacy 57, 75, 127
emotional pain 12
emotional resilience *see* resilience
empathy 13, 37
empowerment 34–5
encopresis 6
enuresis 6
environmental risks 67
Equality Act (2010) 119–20, 124, 136, 142
ESP *see* Education Support Partnership
Every Child Matters 111, 122
exclusion 8, 27, 46, 51, 59, 86
Extended Schools and Health Services 120, 124
eye movement de-sensitisation re-processing 12–13

faecal soiling 6
Family Assessment Framework (FCAF) 58, 59, 108, 111
family mental health 102–3, 104
    engaging families in positive school climate
        110–11
    importance of interagency approach 111–12
    interventions and therapy 13
    maternal mental health 105, 108–10
    paternal mental health 105, 106–8, 109–10
    prevalence and common difficulties 104–5
    protective factors 109–10
    siblings 104–5
    see also parents, carers and families
Farah, Mo 69
Farrell, M. 36
fears 7
feedback boxes 75
fight, flight or freeze 46
FitforWork 142
Fletcher, R. et al. 106–7
foster carers see parents, carers and families
Freeth, R. 12
Frith, E. 38
Fuller, A. 68
'Future in Mind' 3, 4, 15, 31, 119, 121, 134

Gardner, H. 140
Garner, R. 135
gender
    and body image 92, 94
    and bullying 88, 89
    discrimination 119
    and parental mental health 105
Gilmour, J. et al. 8
Goleman, D. 76, 140
Good Childhood Report 65–6, 85, 92
Green, H. et al. 121
Greenberg, M. 121, 122
growth mind-set 35
Gueldner, B. 122

Harewood, T. et al. 106
Haskayne, M. 53
headaches 6
Health and Safety Executive 142
Healthy Schools 35
Hewitt, S. et al. 97
home visits 50, 125
homophobia 28, 86
House of Commons Health Committee 3
humanistic approaches 13
hyperactivity 8, 9
hyperkinetic disorder 9

ICD-10 see International Classification of Diseases
ill health retirement 144
impulsiveness 8, 9
inattention 8, 9
inclusion 117–18

benefits of inclusivity 123–4
defined 119
importance of schools 121–3
inclusive practice in schools 36, 51
    access strategies 127
    case studies 123–4, 125
    classroom culture 126
    defined 119–20
    graduated response 126–8
    school-based support or referrals 127–8
    strategies 124–8
    teaching styles and methods 126–7
    whole school policy 124
independence 7
induction meetings 51
interagency approach 14, 39–40, 50, 111–12, 141–2
International Classification of Diseases (ICD-10)
    6, 7, 9
internet safety 87, 88–90
interventions 12–19
isolation 6

Jacobs Foundation 65

Kanners Syndrome see autistic spectrum conditions
Katz, A. 90
key workers 46

labelling 14
leadership 28, 29–31, 136–8
learning difficulties 9
Li, Q. 88
literacy 33
Livingstone, S. 89
Local Government Pension Scheme 144
looked after children 7, 39, 65, 72–3
Luxmoore, N. 64, 65

management 28, 29–31, 136–8
maternal mental health 105
    anxiety 109, 110
    and attachment 109
    and domestic violence and abuse 109
    perinatal problems 108
    postnatal depression 108, 109
    protective factors 109–10
May, T. 4
mealtimes 54
medicalisation of mental health conditions 4, 5
Mental Health First Aid training 4
Mental Health Foundation 73, 142
mental health in children and young people 1–2, 4–5
    and context 5–6, 13, 15
    developmental perspectives 5, 6, 7
    'good mental health' 73
    origin of problems 4
    prevalence of disorders 4, 45, 47, 119, 121, 122, 135
    terminology 5
    typical problems 5–12

mental health problems in teachers and staff 134–5
Merrell, K. 122
Mind 37, 110, 142, 143
Mind Infoline 143
MindEd 3–4, 38, 92
mindfulness 13, 57, 140–1
mindsets 87–8
mood changes 5, 6
Mosley, J. 76, 77
motivation
    of children 66, 70, 97, 126
    of teachers and staff 140
multiple intelligences 140
Murray, L. *et al.* 109
music, art, design 33
Music, G. 64
Muslim children 86

National Advisory Group 93
National Association of Head Teachers (NAHT)
    135, 136
National Children's Bureau 91
National College for Teaching and Leadership (NCTL) 95
National Foundation for Educational Research (NFER) 135
National Institute for Health and Care Excellence
    (NICE) 7, 104, 141
National Service Framework 4, 119
National Union of Teachers 86
NCB/ASCL 26
neurodevelopmental conditions 120
    see also ADHD; autistic spectrum conditions
Newman, T. 74
'No Health Without Mental Health' strategy 3
nurture clubs 75
nurture groups 13–14, 32, 53–5, 128

obsessive compulsive disorder 7
Ofsted 33
    on CPD 37–8
    No Place for Bullying 87
    on nurture groups 54
    on partnerships 39, 50
    on positive body image 94
    School Inspection Handbook 28, 86
open door policy 32, 50
oppositional defiant disorder 7
out of school activities 36
outside agency support for schools 14, 39–40, 50,
    59, 111–12, 141–2

pain 12
panic disorder 7
parent–infant psychotherapy 13
Parent Partnership 39
Parent Support Advisors 50
parental criminality 8, 11
parents, carers and families
    barriers to relationships 50–3
    and child's self-esteem 77–8

and conduct disorders 8
domestic violence and abuse 11, 107, 109
family breakdown and problems 11, 45, 67
home visits 50, 125
partnership 39–40, 50
positive parenting 78
see also family mental health
paternal mental health 105
    case study 107–8
    depression 109
    and domestic violence and abuse 109
    and possible impact on child 106–7
    postnatal depression 106
    protective factors 109–10
Pearce, J. 67
peer mentoring
    for children 13–14, 36–7
    for teachers and staff 140
peer pressure 26
peer relationships 27
Pelka, Daniel 107
perfectionism 10
performance anxiety 7
person-centred approach 12–13
Personal Education Plans (PEP) 73
personal, social, citizenship and health education
    (PSCHE) co-ordinator 75
personal, social, health and economic education *see*
    PSHE (personal, social, health and economic)
    education
Phippen, A. 90
phobias 7
physical education 33
physical violence 11, 65, 107, 109
'Pitmaston Powers' 95–6
Place2Be 75, 96
play 5, 10, 13, 72
positive parenting 78
positive well-being 29
post-traumatic stress disorder 6, 7, 12
poverty 11
praise 15, 18, 53, 54, 75, 76, 78
prejudice 86, 87
'Prevent' strategy 37, 38, 86
Prever, M. 12
problem-solving skills 34
Professionals Online Safety Helpline 89
PRU (Pupil Referral Units) 59
PSCHE (personal, social, citizenship and health
    education) co-ordinator 75
PSHE Association 34, 75, 92, 94
PSHE (personal, social, health and economic)
    education 33, 34–5, 74–5
    and body image 93–5
    circle time 13, 32, 33–4, 54, 75, 76–7, 126
    promoting positive mental health 75
    social and emotional aspects of learning (SEAL)
        34, 57, 75–6, 122, 126
Ten Principles 93

psychosocial therapies 13
psychotherapy 15–16
Public Health England 27, 28, 30, 32, 37
Public Sector Equality Duty 142
punishment for poor behaviour 4–5, 46
Pupil Referral Units (PRU) 59
puppets 34
Pursuit of Happiness report 3, 15

Quality First Teaching (QFT) 57, 126
quiet areas 32

race and ethnicity 28, 86, 105, 119
Ramchandani, P. *et al.* 106–7
rejection 46
relationships 36, 48
    barriers 50–3
    difficulties 6, 11
    as protective factor 72–3
    and sense of self 64
religious discrimination 86, 119
religious education 33
resilience 83–4
    and bullying 87–8
    case study 95–6
    educational resilience 74
    emotional resilience 97
    importance of 67–9, 122
    role of the school 3, 15–26, 33–4, 73–4
    of teachers and staff 139–41
    see also risk and resilience model
respect 32, 48, 86
risk and resilience model 67–8
risk-taking behaviours 5
Robinson, C. 35
Rogers, C. 13
role play 34
Royal College of Nursing 15
Royal College of Paediatrics and Child Health 4
Royal College of Psychiatrists 11, 86
Rutter, M. 67, 68, 72, 122

sadness 6
safeguarding 37, 89, 95
safety 86
Samaritans 142
school-based counselling 15
school councils 36
school ethos, culture and environment 32–3, 51, 137
    engaging families 110–11
    language 93
    openness 93
    and positive body image 91–5
school governors 30, 31
school level agreements (SLA) 141
school nurses 15
SEAL *see* social and emotional aspects of learning
SEBD *see* social, emotional and behavioural difficulties
self-assessment and improvement tool 30–1

self-awareness 74, 76, 140
self-belief 74, 97
self-concept 74
self-efficacy 64–5
    case study 70–2
    creative curriculum approach 97
    defined 97
    of teachers 97, 141
    value of 70–2, 74
    and voice 35
self-esteem 62–3
    and anorexia nervosa 10
    case study 49
    in the classroom 126
    defined 64–6
    importance of resilience 67–9
    importance of self-esteem 66–7, 91
    PSHE curriculum 74–7
    role of the school 32, 73–4
    within school and community 72–3
    self-efficacy 70–2
    and self-harm 11
    strategies 36, 54, 78
    of teachers 78–9
    therapeutic support 72–3
    working with parents 77–8
self-harm 6, 11–12, 26–7
self, sense of 32, 46, 64–5
self-worth 64
Sellgren, K. 47
SENCos (special educational needs co-ordinators)
    51, 121, 127
SEND (special educational needs and disabilities) 119
    Code of Practice (SEND CoP) 56–9, 120, 124, 127
    school policy 91
SEND Support 56–7, 127
separation anxiety 6, 7
Serious Case Reviews 107
sex and relationship education (SRE) 34
sex discrimination 119–20
sexting 89
sexual abuse 10, 37, 38, 65
sexuality difficulties 11
Sharples, M. *et al.* 88
siblings 104–5
skills 69
SLA (school level agreements) 141
sleep disturbances 6
Smith, P. *et al.* 88
Smith, R.S. 68
social and emotional aspects of learning (SEAL) 34,
    57, 75–6, 122, 126
social and emotional skills 36, 73
social anxiety 7
social disadvantage 45, 51, 104, 108
social, emotional and behavioural difficulties
    (SEBD) 36, 38, 45–7, 53–5
social media 83–4, 89
    and cyberbullying 26–7, 37, 89

impact on body image 91–3
and internet safety 87, 88–90
and peer pressure 26
social, moral, spiritual and cultural (SMSC)
    provision 33–4
social skills 57, 127–8
social withdrawal 6
social workers, partnership with 39
somatic problems 6
South West Grid for Learning 90
special educational needs and disability see SENCos
    (special educational needs
    co-ordinators); SEND
spiral curriculum 34
SRE (sex and relationship education) 34
stigma of mental health 11, 29, 74, 104–5, 122, 134–5, 136
Stirling, S. 27, 30–1
stories and storytelling 75
strategies 12–19
stress
    fight, flight or freeze 46
    signs of stress 137
stress in the workplace 3
    advocacy support 143
    audits 138
    case studies 138–9, 143
    current situation 134–6
    ill health retirement 144
    major components 134
    outside agency support 141–2
    reasonable adjustments 142–3
    return to work 142–3
    role of leaders 136–8
    signs of stress 137
    support levels 135–6, 137
    workload demands 135
substance misuse 6, 7, 9, 11, 107
success, celebrating 50
Sugg, Zoe (Zoella) 92
suicidal behaviour 6, 11–12, 26–7

talents 69
Targeting Mental Health in Schools (TaMHS) 14, 122
Teacher Support Network 59
teachers and staff 132–3
    continuing professional development 37–8, 51, 139
    ill health retirement 144
    inclusive practice 126–7
    levels of retention 86
    mental health problems 134–5
    mentors for 38
    mindfulness 13, 57, 140–1
    open door policy 32
    peer mentoring 140
    physical, emotional, mental health 32
    resilience and well-being 139–41
    self-efficacy 97, 141
    self-esteem 78–9
    supervision 140

support networks 8, 59, 139, 140
    training 85–6, 139
    work–life balance 79, 136, 139, 140
    see also stress in the workplace
Teachers' Pension Scheme 144
Teachers' Standards 79, 140
teaching styles and methods 126–7
teaching unions 142
teamwork 33, 51
tearfulness and crying 6, 137
therapeutic treatment approaches 12–19, 72–3
Think Family 111–12
Time to Change 106, 142
Together We Stand 121
tummy aches 6
Tyers, C. et al. 134

UN Convention on the Rights of the Child
    (UNCRC) 5, 35, 91
unconditional positive regard 13
UNESCO 120
UNICEF 65

voice of children and young people 35–7, 70, 91, 94, 126

'wave model' of intervention 56–7, 73–4
Weare, K. 14, 27, 28, 29, 30, 32, 33, 34, 35, 36, 39,
    47, 51, 65, 73, 79, 110, 121–2, 137, 139
weight loss 6
well-being 29, 65–6, 87, 141
Werner, E. 68
whole school approach 24–5, 26–9, 29f
    behaviour policy 47–59
    bullying policy 28, 30, 34, 87, 91
    circle time 13, 76–7
    curriculum planning and practice 33–5
    inclusive practice 124
    leadership and management 28, 29–31, 136–8
    need for 26–8
    partnership with parents, carers and outside
        agencies 14, 39–40, 50, 111–12, 141–2
    positive well-being 29
    resilience 3, 15–26, 33–4, 73–4
    school ethos, culture and environment 32–3, 51,
        91–5, 110–11, 137
    self-assessment and improvement tool 30–1
    staff and continuing professional development
        37–8, 51, 139
    voice of children and young people 35–7
withdrawn children 16–17, 27, 47
work–life balance 79, 136, 139, 140
World Health Organisation 135
worry boxes 32, 95
Wyn, J. et al. 27

Yeager, D. 87–8
Young Minds 65, 66–7
Youth Wellbeing Directory 40
YouTube 92